AS/A-LEVEL

19th & 20th Century
European &
World History

Derrick Murphy

ESSENTIAL WORD
DICTIONARY

Philip Allan Updates
Market Place
Deddington
Oxfordshire
OX15 0SE

Tel: 01869 338652
Fax: 01869 337590
e-mail: sales@philipallan.co.uk
www.philipallan.co.uk

ISBN 0 86003 378 3

Acknowledgements
My thanks to Brother John Sreenan OBE.

P00094

Printed by Raithby, Lawrence & Co Ltd, Leicester

Introduction

This *Essential Word Dictionary* will provide you with invaluable information to use as you prepare for the AS or A2 examinations. (The specific modules/units covered are listed in an appendix — see pages 161–164.) To succeed at these examinations you need to:

- have a sound **knowledge and understanding of history**. This means being able to recall, select and deploy historical knowledge accurately.
- be able to evaluate **sources in historical context**. This means having knowledge of the topic on which the source is based.
- be able to explain **different historical interpretations.** A new feature of A2 History is **synoptic assessment**. This involves bringing together in one answer different aspects of history. One of these aspects could be the role of the individual.
- display good written communication skills. This is also an important part of **Basic Key Skills**, and includes the ability to use historical terms accurately.

This dictionary will enable you to deal effectively with all these features of the AS and A2 examinations. Included in the dictionary are entries on:

- major historical events such as wars and treaties.
- important historical terms such as balance of power.
- key historical figures.

The dictionary can be used:

- to define historical terms. These are required in dealing with document questions and in extended writing such as essays.
- to help you to understand a particular topic.
- as a revision aid.

To use the dictionary as a revision aid, first compile a checklist of essential terms, events and individuals you need for an examination. Look these terms up in the dictionary and then learn and understand them so that you can use them with confidence in the examination.

Each entry is broken down into a maximum of three parts:

(1) A simple definition is given after the headword.
(2) This is followed by a series of bullet points which place important events in historical context.
(3) An examiner's tip is then included where appropriate. These tips are intended to help you to use the entries in your studies. They include references to common misunderstandings about the entry or offer advice on how to use the terms in preparation for examinations.

For each entry it may be necessary to make a cross-reference to the words in italics in order to understand fully the entry you are reading.

This title is one of a series of *Essential Word Dictionaries*, which includes a companion volume on *AS/A-Level 19th and 20th Century British History*.

Abyssinian War, 1935–36: occurred when *fascist* Italy, under *Mussolini,* invaded and conquered the East African state of Abyssinia (Ethiopia). It began with a border incident with Italian Somaliland at Wal Wal.

- The invasion was part of an attempt by Mussolini to establish an East African Italian empire. Italian action was condemned by the *League of Nations*, leading to Italy's withdrawal from that organisation.
- The war also led to the collapse of the *Stresa Front* of Britain, France and Italy against German rearmament.
- An attempt was made to appease Mussolini with the *Hoare–Laval Pact,* but this was rejected by the British and French governments.
- **TIP** This war was important in undermining the authority of the League of Nations; it disrupted opposition to German rearmament; and it helped to push Germany and Italy together as allies.

Acerbo Law: an electoral law passed in 1923 by the Italian Parliament. It stated that any political party gaining 25% of votes at an election would receive two-thirds (66%) of parliamentary seats.

- Its effect was to increase the political control of the *fascist* government under *Mussolini.*
- It was an important step on the road to making Mussolini dictator of Italy.
- **TIP** This law is important in any answer which requires you to explain how Mussolini was able to transform his minority government into a dictatorship.

Adenauer, Konrad: West Germany's first Chancellor, 1949–63.

- He was a leading member of the Catholic Centre Party in the 1920s and an opponent of the Nazis after 1933. He spent 1933–45 either in prison or in hiding.
- He helped create the West German Constitution in 1948–49 and led West Germany into *NATO* in 1955 and the *EEC* in 1957.
- He also established diplomatic relations with the *USSR* in 1955.
- **TIP** Adenauer was committed to ensuring that West Germany was part of the Western military alliance. He also helped lay the foundations for west European economic integration.

Adrianople, Treaty of, 1829: ended the Russo–Turkish War of 1828–29.

- The war guaranteed the independence of Greece from the *Ottoman* (Turkish) *empire*.
- Under the treaty the Turkish provinces of Moldavia and Wallachia (modern Romania) were given autonomy (self-government).
- Russia gained territory, at Turkey's expense, in the Caucasus region between the Black and Caspian seas.
- ■ *TIP* This was the last time Russia and Turkey fought a war without the intervention of the European *Great Powers*. It is important in any answer on international relations of the period or the *Eastern Question*.

Afghanistan, Soviet invasion of, 1979: an occupation by the Soviet Army, to overthrow the government led by Hafizullah Amin.

- The *USSR* wanted a more pro-Soviet government and replaced Amin with Babrak Karmal.
- This intervention was justified in the USSR by the *Brezhnev Doctrine*.
- It aroused fears that the USSR was attempting to extend its influence towards the oil-rich Persian Gulf.
- The invasion resulted in the end of *détente* and the beginning of a new *Cold War*. The US Senate refused to ratify (sign) the *SALT* II Treaty. President *Carter* announced a boycott of the 1980 Moscow Olympic Games by the US team.
- ■ *TIP* Soviet intervention led to a 10-year war with Afghan rebels, and eventually to Soviet withdrawal and defeat of the pro-Soviet Afghan government.

African National Congress (ANC): an anti-racist political organisation formed in 1910.

- It opposed the racist policies of White South African governments from the creation of the Union of South Africa in 1910. The ANC was a leading opponent of the policy of *apartheid*, which was introduced by the South African government in 1948.
- Its most important leader was Nelson Mandela. Following the Sharpeville massacre of 1960 Mandela supported armed resistance to apartheid. He was arrested and imprisoned from 1963 to 1993. He led the ANC to power as the first multiracial government in a democratic Republic of South Africa.
- ■ *TIP* Do not confuse ANC with PAC (Pan-Africanist Congress), which organised the Sharpeville demonstration and was in favour of Black African, not multiracial, government.

Agadir Crisis, 1911: an attempt by Germany to force France to hand over parts of the French Congo to the German empire (also known as the Second Moroccan Crisis).

- It led Britain openly to threaten war against Germany through mobilising the Royal Navy's Home Fleet in the North Sea.
- Britain and France were brought closer together in a common fear of German colonial ambitions.
- ■ *TIP* This crisis was an important event in pushing Britain and France towards conflict with Germany.

Agent Orange: a chemical defoliant used by US forces in the *Vietnam War* in an attempt to uncover *Vietcong* military and supply movements.

- In 'Operation Ranch Hand' large amounts of dioxin-based Agent Orange were dropped across South Vietnam.
- It had very limited impact on Vietcong movements, but was an ecological disaster. Large areas of forest were destroyed. Agent Orange entered the water table and resulted in birth defects among Vietnamese children and livestock.
- *TIP* This was the most extensive use of chemical warfare since the First World War and fuelled opposition to US involvement in the war both at home and abroad.

Agricultural Adjustment Act, 1933: an attempt to increase farmers' incomes during the first *New Deal*.

- The US government planned to subsidise farmers who voluntarily reduced their production, thereby cutting supply.
- The Agricultural Adjustment Administration (AAA) agreed to pay farmers to reduce production of major crops such as grain, milk and pigs. In the event, a reduction in production was aided by droughts.
- Over 75 million acres (40 million hectares) were taken out of production by 1935. Farm incomes rose by $2.9 billion.
- *TIP* The AAA was criticised for destroying food while the unemployed went hungry. In fact it only destroyed cotton and pigs.

Aix-la-Chapelle Congress, 1818: the first meeting of the *Great Powers* following the Congress of Vienna, 1814–15.

- Importantly, it allowed France to join the *Congress System*. The *Quadruple Alliance* of 1815 of Austria, Prussia, Russia and Britain became the Quintuple Alliance with the addition of France.
- *TIP* This is the only congress of the Congress System which saw agreement between all Europe's Great Powers.

Alexander I: Russian Emperor (Tsar), 1801–25.

- He was a leading figure in the defeat of Napoleon.
- Noted for his moderate, liberal views on society up to 1815, he later became the main supporter of conservatism in Europe.
- He founded the *Holy Alliance* of 1815, which included most monarchs in Europe. Britain, the Papal States and Ottoman Turkey were not members. The Holy Alliance aimed to prevent liberal revolution against autocratic (dictatorial) monarchs.

Alexander II: Russian Tsar, 1855–81.

- He was known as the 'Tsar Liberator' because he *emancipated the serfs* in 1861. His reign saw major reform across Russian society. He introduced elected local government in 1864, reformed the judicial system in 1870 and reformed the armed forces, introducing conscription.
- During his reign Russia fought Turkey in 1877 and 1878. Russia also expanded its empire into central Asia, capturing Bokhara, Samarkand and Tashkent.

- He was assassinated by 'The People's Will', a terrorist organisation, on his way to sign a decree to allow Russia its first elected national parliament.

Alexander III: Russian Tsar, 1881–94.

- In retaliation for Alexander II's assassination in 1881, he introduced a policy of repression. Land captains were appointed to control the Russian provinces. *Pogroms* (attacks) on Jews were organised by the government. The secret police (*Okhrana*) arrested and imprisoned political opponents of the Tsar. Political parties were banned.
- A policy of *Russification* was introduced, making Russian the official language of the empire.
- In foreign affairs, Alexander III signed a political and military alliance with France in 1893–94, making Russia a potential enemy of Germany and Austria-Hungary. He also expanded Russian control in Asia to the borders of Afghanistan.

Amiens, Peace of, 1802: ended the war between France and Britain which began in 1793.

- It established France as Europe's major power. The King of England gave up his claim to the French throne. In return, Britain kept Ceylon (Sri Lanka) and Trinidad in the West Indies.
- The peace was only a truce in the Napoleonic Wars. Britain refused to give up Malta and French colonies in India.
- War broke out again in 1803.

TIP There was a series of peace treaties during the Napoleonic Wars. Remember, one of Napoleon's aims was to break up coalitions of powers against him. This treaty was part of that process.

ANC: see *African National Congress*.

ancien régime: a term to describe government and society before the French Revolution.

- It was closely associated with rule by an autocratic monarch who claimed authority from God (the Divine Right of Kings).
- It reflected a society dominated by a privileged class of landowners (the aristocracy). The aristocracy also wielded regional power.
- Most of the population were peasants who had to provide services and/or payment to their landowners. (This was known as feudal privileges.)

TIP Most closely associated with France before 1789, the term can be applied to all European states before that date.

Andropov, Yuri: Soviet leader, 1982–83.

- As Soviet ambassador to Hungary he played a leading part in the suppression of the *Hungarian Uprising* in 1956.
- He was chairman of the *KGB*, 1967–82.
- He outmanoeuvred Konstantin *Chernenko* to succeed Leonid *Brezhnev* as Soviet leader in May 1982.
- Though he attempted reform of the *USSR* and increased the influence of Mikhail *Gorbachev* in the Communist Party hierarchy, reformist developments

were limited by his illness and his death in the summer of 1983.

■ *TIP* His brief period in office was an early attempt to reform the USSR's stagnant economy. Plans for this were later put into operation by Gorbachev after 1985.

Anglo–French Naval Agreement, 1912: a secret agreement which was the direct result of the *Agadir Crisis*.

● Britain agreed to defend the North Sea and Channel coastline of both countries in the event of war. France agreed to defend the Mediterranean possessions of both countries.

● This agreement was revealed to the British Cabinet and the House of Commons only at the end of July 1914; it helped force Britain into war with Germany on 4 August.

■ *TIP* The agreement made British entry into a Franco–German war almost inevitable.

Anglo–Japanese Alliance, 1902: the first military alliance signed by Britain since the *Crimean War* (1854–56), it brought to an end the period of *splendid isolation*.

● Britain signed because of fears of German naval rivalry. It allowed Britain to redeploy its naval forces from the Far East to the North Sea. Japan feared Russian ambitions in Korea and northern China.

● Each side agreed to remain neutral if the other power was at war with one country. However, if one of the signatories was at war with more than one country, the other would intervene militarily.

● The alliance prevented French involvement in the *Russo–Japanese War* of 1904–05, but it led to Japan joining Britain and France in the First World War against Germany and Austria-Hungary in 1914.

■ *TIP* This alliance was important in explaining Britain's eventual involvement in the First World War.

Anglo–Russian Entente, 1907: a colonial agreement over Persia (Iran), which created Russian and British zones of influence.

● It brought to an end a period of colonial rivalry between the two countries in central Asia.

● From 1905, Russia and France were in military alliance. Britain and France and Britain and Russia had made colonial agreements called ententes. Contrary to popular belief, no Triple Entente existed before the outbreak of war in 1914.

■ *TIP* It is important to note that this colonial agreement did not commit Britain to any military action in Europe.

annex (vb)**:** to acquire or take over land.

■ *TIP* Use the term when explaining changes brought about by war or treaty. For instance, in 1919 France annexed Alsace-Lorraine.

Anschluss, 1938: the name given to the German take-over ('forcible union') of Austria in March 1938.

● *Hitler* had always wished to unite Austria with Germany. In 1934, Austrian Nazis failed in an attempt to achieve union. This was due, in part, to Italian opposition.

- In March 1938, Hitler was forced into action before the Austrian Chancellor, Kurt von Schussnigg, could call a referendum on Austrian independence. In 1938 *Mussolini* had become Hitler's ally and did not oppose union.
- Neither Britain nor France opposed the Anschluss because of their policy of *appeasement*.
- **■ TIP** The Anschluss was crucial for Hitler in achieving his aim of uniting all German-speaking peoples. It also gave Germany Austria's gold reserves and heavy industry, which helped with German rearmament.

Anti-Comintern Pact, 1937: an international agreement between Germany, Italy and Japan.

- The pact was aimed against the *USSR* and international communism. It followed on from the Axis Agreement of 1936 between Germany and Italy.
- **■ TIP** The pact further developed *Hitler*'s foreign policy. However, Japan never became involved militarily in the Second World War in Europe.

anti-Semitism: a dislike of Jews or the Jewish religion. It has resulted in the persecution of Jews in Europe since medieval times.

- With the rise of nationalism in Europe in the nineteenth century, anti-Semitism took on a new intensity. In particular, it associated nationalist ideas with the racist theories of *Social Darwinism*.
- In France, anti-Semitism revealed itself in the *Panama Scandal* and the *Dreyfus Affair* of the 1890s.
- In Russia in the 1880s, government-sponsored *pogroms* were launched against the Jews.
- The most extreme version of anti-Semitism is linked with *Hitler* and the Nazi Party. Between 1933 and 1939 Jews were denied German citizenship and faced the threat of physical attack. During the Second World War, the Nazis launched the *Final Solution*, a plan to exterminate the entire Jewish population of Europe.
- **■ TIP** Anti-Semitism was a feature of European society throughout the nineteenth and early twentieth centuries.

apartheid: a racist policy of 'apartness' introduced by the Nationalist government of South Africa in 1948.

- The policy built on racist legislation of previous governments, which made sure that Whites dominated South African politics.
- South Africa was divided into four racial groups: Whites, Bantu (Blacks), Asians and Cape Coloured. Apartheid created separate housing, education and transport facilities for each of these groups. In the late 1950s Prime Minister Verwoerd created Bantustans (homelands) for the Black population.
- The ultimate aim was to deny Blacks South African citizenship and an equal vote with Whites. This policy led to an international boycott of South Africa, in particular in sport, from the 1970s to the 1990s.

appeasement: a policy of maintaining peace through making concessions or agreeing with demands.

a

- Appeasement was a foreign policy associated particularly with the governments of Britain and France in the 1930s.
- An attempt to ease international tension and prevent war, it began with Stanley Baldwin's government of 1935–37. The *Hoare–Laval Pact* and the Anglo–German Naval Agreement of 1935 are examples of appeasement.
- The most important act of appeasement was the agreement arising from the *Munich Crisis* of September 1938. British Prime Minister Neville *Chamberlain* and French Prime Minister Edouard Daladier agreed to give *Hitler* the German-speaking *Sudetenland* of Czechoslovakia.
- **TIP** Appeasement is regarded as an important factor in causing the Second World War in Europe. Britain abandoned appeasement in March 1939, when Germany occupied the Czech-speaking provinces of Bohemia and Moravia in Czechoslovakia.

April Theses, 1917: a statement made by the *Bolshevik* leader, *Lenin*, on his return to Russia from exile.
- It shocked Bolshevik supporters by suggesting that the Bolsheviks should overthrow the newly created *Provisional Government*.
- It led to two failed attempts, in June and July 1917, to overthrow the Provisional Government through street demonstrations.
- Lenin then encouraged Bolshevik participation in the All-Russia *Soviet* and in local soviets. He also suggested, and led, the Bolshevik seizure of power through the *October Revolution of 1917*.
- **TIP** The April Theses is an important landmark in the causes of the Bolshevik (communist) seizure of power in 1917. It ensured Lenin's leadership of the Bolsheviks and distanced the Bolsheviks from other Russian socialists, such as the *Mensheviks*.

armistice: a cease-fire.
- The most famous armistice was signed on 11 November 1918. Although fighting came to an end, the First World War was not officially declared over until the signing of the Treaty of *Versailles* by Germany on 28 June 1919.

Article 48: an important section of the *Weimar* Constitution of 1919.
- It gave the German president the authority to appoint and sack chancellors if no one political party had majority support in the *Reichstag* (lower house of the national parliament).
- The article was used by President *Hindenburg* to appoint the last four chancellors of the Weimar Republic: *Brüning*, von Papen, von Schleicher and *Hitler*.
- **TIP** This article is important because it supports the view that Hitler was legally appointed Chancellor on 30 January 1933. It can thus be claimed that Hitler did not seize power, he was given it.

assignat: paper money issued during the French Revolution.
- Begun in 1790 as a method of granting citizens former Church land or part of the national debt, the move to introduce assignats was supported by the *Jacobins*. During the revolution the value of assignats dropped considerably.

Atlantic Charter, 1941: an agreement of principles between Britain and the USA made in August 1941, 4 months before America entered the war.

● Both countries agreed to support free international trade, democracy, freedom of the seas and disarmament.

● The charter formed the basis of the *United Nations* Charter of 1945.

▪ *TIP* The Atlantic Charter is important because, along with *lend-lease*, it showed that the American government was a strong supporter of Britain in the Second World War before *Pearl Harbor.*

atomic bomb: brought the Pacific War with Japan to an end in 1945.

● First developed by the USA in the Manhattan Project during the Second World War, the incentive to produce the bomb was the fear that Nazi Germany was developing a similar device.

● It was tested successfully in July 1945, 2 months after the end of the war with Germany.

● President *Truman* decided to use the bomb against Japan. The plan was to end the Pacific War quickly, before the *USSR* could intervene. It was preferred over a mainland invasion of Japan, thus saving the lives of thousands of Allied troops. Two bombs were dropped in August 1945, on the cities of Hiroshima and Nagasaki, resulting in over 120,000 deaths.

● The Japanese surrendered on 2 September. The after-effects of radiation killed thousands more Japanese civilians.

▪ *TIP* These cataclysmic events began the nuclear age. By 2000 the USA, Britain, France, Russia, Ukraine, India, Pakistan and communist China had all become official nuclear powers. Israel and South Africa also possessed nuclear weapons.

Ausgleich, 1867: a change ('compromise') in the constitution and structure of the Habsburg empire.

● The change was made to accommodate Hungarian opposition to the empire.

● From 1867 onwards the empire was divided into two self-governing states, Austria and Hungary. Each part had its own government and parliament.

● The new empire of Austria-Hungary also had a federal government in charge of foreign and military affairs.

▪ *TIP* From 1867 Austria-Hungary could also be known as the Habsburg (or Hapsburg) Monarchy, the Dual Monarchy or the Danube Monarchy.

Austerlitz, Battle of, 1805: one of *Napoleon's* greatest military victories, in which he defeated the armies of Austria, Prussia and Russia.

● This victory destroyed the third *Coalition against Napoleon.*

● In the Peace of Pressburg, after the battle, Austria lost territory to Bavaria and the Kingdom of Italy.

● In 1806 Napoleon abolished the Holy Roman Empire, of which the Austrian Habsburgs had been emperors for nearly 400 years.

autarky: a concept meaning economic self-sufficiency, particularly associated with *Hitler's* economic policy.

- Hitler regarded the British economic blockade of 1914–18 as an important factor in Germany's defeat.
- In the 1930s the Nazis attempted to make their economy self-sufficient in war. The Four Year Plan of 1936 aimed to achieve autarky. The manufacture of synthetic rubber and hydrogeneration (making oil from coal) were important parts of this plan.
- *TIP* Autarky was a critical policy goal for both Nazi Germany and fascist Italy. It is closely associated with creating a war economy.

Autobahnen: the German motorway system begun by the Nazis in the 1930s.

- Motorway building used tens of thousands of formerly unemployed workers. It not only helped reduce unemployment, but was also a prestige project which the Nazis exploited for propaganda purposes.
- It gave Germany a modern transport network — very useful in wartime.
- *TIP* This programme was a major project for the RAD (*Reichsarbeitsdienst*), or National Labour Service, the organisation set up to help reduce unemployment.

autonomous: a term used to describe regions or areas within a country or empire which control their own internal affairs.

- In Britain, Scotland has achieved a measure of autonomy since devolution.
- After the *Ausgleich* of 1867, Hungary achieved autonomy.
- In the *USSR* each separate republic, such as the Ukraine or Georgia, was autonomous. In the USA states such as New York and California are self-governing.
- *TIP* The term usually applies to areas within a state or empire, but generally excludes foreign policy. Some states control the foreign policy of other states. This is known as suzerainty.

Bagration, Operation, 1944: a major *Red Army* offensive in Belorussia against German Army Group Centre.

- This took place at the same time as the *D-Day* invasion in the West. The Red Army all but destroyed Army Group Centre and liberated western Russia and eastern Poland as a result.

■ *TIP* After this defeat the German Army on the Eastern Front never recovered.

balance of power: a term used in international relations, referring in particular to military power.

- From the eighteenth to the twentieth centuries, European statesmen attempted to create, and then maintain, a balance of power, intending that no country should dominate the continent.
- A balance was secured by the Treaty of *Vienna* (1814–15) and by the Treaty of *Versailles* (1919). Occasionally countries attempted to destroy the balance of power, to their own advantage. This happened in France under *Napoleon* and in Germany in both 1914 and the 1930s.
- From 1945 to 1991 a global balance existed between the USA and the *USSR*. With the advance of nuclear weapons this also became a balance of terror.

■ *TIP* Most studies of international relations from 1789 onwards require discussion of this concept. It is associated with the *Congress System* (1815–25) and the *Concert of Europe* (1815–1914).

Balkans: the Balkans peninsula in southeastern Europe today comprises Greece, Macedonia, Serbia, Montenegro, Albania, Bulgaria, Romania, Croatia and part of Turkey.

- For much of the nineteenth century it was part of the *Ottoman* (Turkish) *empire*, which was then in decline. It was regarded as an area of possible Russian and Austrian expansion.
- The chief development in the nineteenth century was the rise of nationalism among the Balkan peoples. Between 1815 and 1914 Greece, Romania and Bulgaria were created. Serbia ceased to be an *autonomous* part of the Ottoman empire and became the largest Balkan state. Conflicts between Balkan states and Turkey resulted in wars during the nineteenth and early twentieth centuries, culminating in the *Balkan Wars* of 1912–13 and the *July Crisis* of 1914.

■ *TIP* This was a major area of political instability in Europe from 1815 to 1914 — and again in the 1990s with the collapse of Yugoslavia.

Balkan Wars, 1912–13: local conflicts, which became an important prelude to the First World War.

- In the First Balkan War, the Balkan League of Serbia, Bulgaria, Greece and Montenegro defeated the *Ottoman* (Turkish) *empire*.
- The Second Balkan War was mainly between Serbia and Bulgaria, due to disagreements over the Treaty of London (1913), which ended the First War.
- The two Balkan Wars were important in explaining the outbreak of the First World War. As a result of the wars Serbia became the strongest Balkan state. By early 1914 it was seen by Austria-Hungary as a major threat to its position in southeast Europe.
- When Archduke Franz Ferdinand was assassinated at *Sarajevo* by a Bosnian Serb, Austria-Hungary used the opportunity to begin what it thought would be a victorious Third Balkan War. By August 1914 this war had escalated into the First World War.

Banking Act, 1935: an attempt by the federal government to control the US banking industry.

- The act greatly increased the power of the Federal Reserve Board.
- The original Federal Reserve Act of 1913 had allowed individual state reserve banks. However, the act forced all banks seeking new federal deposit insurance to register with the Federal Reserve Board and accept its control over the banking system.

■ *TIP* This was a key component of the second *New Deal*. The act followed other banking reforms of *Roosevelt*'s, which included the *Emergency Banking Relief Act* and the *Glass–Steagall Banking Act*, both in 1933.

Bao Dai: the last Emperor of Vietnam.

- He was used by the French as a puppet head of state. Crowned in 1925 at the age of 12, he remained Emperor until the demise of French rule in 1954.
- After partition of Vietnam as a result of the *Geneva Accords* of 1954, Bao Dai became Emperor of South Vietnam. He made Ngo Dinh *Diem* his Prime Minister and Diem took effective control of South Vietnam after the 1956 election. Thereafter Bao Dai ceased to have any influence in politics.

■ *TIP* Bao Dai was an indolent playboy, used by the French and by Diem for their own political purposes.

Barbarossa, Operation, 1941: the code name for the invasion in June of the *USSR* by Germany, Romania, Hungary and Finland.

- This was the greatest land invasion of all time. *Hitler* hoped to destroy the Soviet Union by *blitzkrieg* within 6 months.
- Hitler wished to destroy communism and create *Lebensraum* (living space) for the German population in eastern Europe.
- The attack led to the conquest of most of the western part of the USSR, but was stopped initially at the Battle of Moscow in December 1941.

battle for grain: an attempt by *Mussolini*'s *fascist* government to increase grain production in the 1920s and 1930s.

- By 1939 grain production was twice that of 1922, but Italy still had to import grain. The 'battle' was used for propaganda purposes by the fascists. Its most notable achievement was the draining of the Pontine marshes near Rome.

▧ *TIP* Mussolini's 'battles' were an important part of his domestic policy and propaganda. This one should be linked with the battle for births (to increase the Italian population) and the battle for land (to redistribute land). Both these projects failed to meet their targets.

Bay of Pigs, 1961: an American attempt, sponsored by the *CIA*, to overthrow Fidel *Castro* with an invasion by Cuban exiles.

- The invasion was organised during the last days of the *Eisenhower* administration, but was supported by *Kennedy* on becoming President of the USA in January 1961.
- The operation was badly planned and the Cuban exiles had poor weaponry. Kennedy cancelled air support at the last minute.
- Over 1,200 exiles were captured by Castro's troops, who had been armed by the *USSR*.

▧ *TIP* The fiasco led to a rapid deterioration in US–Cuban relations, forcing Castro firmly into the Soviet camp. It was followed by Cuba's decision to allow Soviet nuclear weapons to be placed on the island, precipitating the *Cuban Missile Crisis*. It caused massive embarrassment for the Kennedy administration.

Beer Hall Putsch, 1923: an attempt by *Hitler* to seize power in Munich, Bavaria, as a prelude to marching on Berlin to overthrow the *Weimar* government and make former Field Marshal von *Ludendorff* dictator.

- The attempt failed, mainly because the Munich Chief of Police refused to support the Nazis. Hitler's followers were dispersed by armed police; 16 were killed.
- Hitler was sentenced to 5 years in prison, but served only 9 months. During his time in prison he wrote *Mein Kampf* ('My Struggle').

▧ *TIP* This event is also known as the Munich Putsch. A *putsch* is a failed attempt to seize power. The episode led to a complete change in Hitler's tactics to gain power. From 1925 onwards he began to drop his socialist ideas, to concentrate on nationalism and anti-communism.

Belgian Revolt, 1830–39: a Belgian uprising against rule by the king of Holland in a United Netherlands.

- This led to the first major revision of the Treaty of *Vienna, 1814–15.*
- The *Holy Alliance* powers of Austria, Russia and Prussia wanted to crush the revolt, but were distracted by the *Polish Revolt* of 1830–31, which affected their own territory.
- Belgian independence was agreed by the Treaty of London (1839).
- It was brought about mainly through the efforts of the British Foreign Secretary, Lord *Palmerston*. He wanted to create an independent Belgian state, free from

French influence and friendly towards Britain. The latter aim was achieved by having Queen Victoria's uncle, Leopold, accepted as Belgium's first king.

■ *TIP* The creation of Belgian independence is a good example of the *Concert of Europe* in operation. Major war was avoided and Belgium was guaranteed independence by Europe's five *Great Powers*. When Germany attacked Belgium in 1914 Britain used the event to declare war on Germany, because it broke the Treaty of London.

Beria, Lavrenti: head of the *NKVD* from 1938 to 1953.

● He expanded the role of the Soviet Secret Police and played a major part in organising the Soviet war effort during the Second World War. He was made a Marshal of the Soviet Union in 1945.

● He influenced development of the *Gulag* concentration-camp system and was important in establishing communist rule in eastern Europe.

● On *Stalin's* death (1953) he attempted to bring all police authority under his control, but was outmanoeuvred by Malenkov and *Khrushchev*. He was arrested and shot.

■ *TIP* Beria was a leading henchman of Stalin during the final year of the Great *Purge* and during the Second World War.

Berlin, Treaty of, 1878: the result of the Congress of Berlin on the *Eastern Question*, with Bismarck acting as 'honest broker' between Britain, Austria-Hungary, Russia and the *Ottoman* (Turkish) *empire*.

● It altered the Treaty of *San Stefano* (1878). Bulgaria was divided into three: part was returned to Turkey, part remained the new state of Bulgaria, and part became the self-governing province of Eastern Roumelia within the Ottoman empire.

● The treaty preserved the European *balance of power* and brought a brief period of stability in the *Balkans*, which lasted until the *Bulgarian Crisis* of 1885–87.

■ *TIP* This treaty forms an important part of any study of *Bismarck's* foreign policy, British foreign policy and the Eastern Question.

Berlin, Treaty of, 1926: between the *USSR* and Germany, confirming the Treaty of Rapallo of 1922.

● The initiative for this treaty came from the USSR. In return for supporting them in the *League of Nations*, Germany received loans from the USSR.

● Both parties were also committed to neutrality and opposed to the boycott of any country.

■ *TIP* This was an example of how the USSR sought foreign support in a period when it feared intervention from the Western capitalist world in Soviet affairs.

Berlin Airlift Crisis, 1948–49: a major conflict between the *USSR* and the Western Allies, which began with a Soviet blockade of land routes across East Germany, from West Germany to West Berlin, and resulted in a massive airlift of supplies.

● The Soviet Union decided to take action following the Allied decision to create a single currency for their areas of (West) Germany.

- Stalin ended the blockade in June 1949, when it was apparent that the Allies had no intention of abandoning West Berlin.
- The crisis was the first major success for the US policy of *containment* against the USSR. It led directly to the creation of *NATO* in 1949.
- **TIP** Make sure you refer to the policy of containment when writing about this crisis.

Berlin Decrees, 1806: established the *Continental blockade* whereby *Napoleon* attempted to stop Europe trading with Britain.

- They were extended with the Milan Decrees in 1807.
- Britain retaliated with an Order in Council, forbidding trade with neutral countries which accepted the Berlin Decrees.
- This started a trade war between Britain and French-controlled Europe.

Berlin Wall Crisis, 1961: began in August when East German troops built a wall separating East from West Berlin.

- The Berlin Wall filled the last gap in the *Iron Curtain* between East and West. The wall was a major source of conflict in the *Cold War*. The Soviet leader, *Khrushchev*, had attempted to force the Western Allies out of Berlin since 1958.
- Khrushchev decided to act because he regarded the American President, John F. *Kennedy*, as weak and indecisive following the *Bay of Pigs* fiasco in April 1961.
- **TIP** The crisis should be seen as an important event in forcing Kennedy to make a strong stand against Soviet nuclear missiles in Cuba in October 1962.

Bethmann-Hollweg, Theobald: appointed German Chancellor (1909–17) following the dismissal of von Bulow.

- He faced diplomatic isolation abroad, witnessing the growth of friendship between Britain, France and Russia. At home, the rise in popularity of the *Social Democrat Party* began to cause concern in the government.
- He attended the *War Cabinet Meeting* of 8 December 1912, where German leaders openly discussed the idea of a European war to solve Germany's foreign and domestic problems.
- After the outbreak of war in 1914, Bethmann-Hollweg's influence declined. By the end of 1916 the Army High Command was making most major political decisions.
- **TIP** He was a leading German political figure in the decision to risk war in 1914 to solve Germany's domestic and foreign problems.

Bismarck, Otto von: a leading figure in making Prussia the dominant power in Germany and in making Germany a strong and united nation; Prussian Minister-President 1862–90; Chancellor of Germany 1871–90.

- He helped isolate Austria in the war of 1866 through developing friendly relations with France and Russia, and led Prussia to victory in the *Franco–Prussian War* of 1870–71.
- He helped create the German empire (*Second Reich*) in 1871 and wrote the German Constitution, which lasted from 1871 to 1918.

- Dominating European international relations from 1871 to 1890 through a series of agreements and alliances with Europe's major states, Bismarck's main aim was to isolate France. He feared Catholics and socialists within Germany as threats to Prussian dominance.
- The Emperor dismissed Bismarck from power in 1890 because he suggested introducing martial law and suspending the Constitution.
- **TIP** Bismarck dominated European affairs from 1862 to 1890. Be aware that recent historical interpretations downplay Bismarck's role in German unification. They point to economic integration and nationalism as other important factors.

Black Sea Clauses, 1856: the most important parts of the Treaty of *Paris*, which brought an end to the *Crimean War*.

- They declared that Russia was forbidden to build a fleet in the Black Sea. This was Britain's main war aim.
- They helped maintain British naval dominance in the eastern Mediterranean. In 1870, at the height of the *Franco–Prussian War*, Russia revoked (rejected) the clauses. Britain accepted Russia's decision in the Treaty of London (1870).
- **TIP** An important feature of the *Eastern Question* throughout the nineteenth century was Britain's fear of a Russian naval presence in the Mediterranean.

Blanc, Louis: French socialist who helped bring down the regime of King *Louis Philippe* in 1848.

- He supported political and social reform. In a period of economic crisis in early 1848 he helped establish *National Workshops*, a form of unemployment relief.
- When these were abandoned in June there was an armed uprising of Parisian workers, which was defeated.

blitzkrieg: a 'lightning war' of fast-moving land assaults, associated with Germany between 1939 and 1941.

- Based on the mass use of tanks and armoured vehicles supported by air cover, it was adopted by the Germans because they lacked the economic capacity to fight long wars.
- The tactic was employed very successfully against Poland in 1939, against France and the Low Countries in the summer of 1940, and against Yugoslavia and Greece in the spring of 1941.
- The greatest example was *Operation Barbarossa*, against the Soviet Union in the second half of 1941. It was spectacularly successful until December 1941, when the German attack was repulsed outside Moscow.
- **TIP** An important factor in *Hitler*'s early successes in the Second World War, the technique effectively combined the new technology of armoured vehicles with air power.

Blomberg–Fritsch Affair, 1938: an episode which led to *Hitler* becoming Commander-in-Chief of the German armed forces (**Wehrmacht**).

- Field Marshal von Blomberg was Minister of War and Werner von Fritsch was the commander of the German Army. According to police records, it was

b

revealed that Era Gruhn, Blomberg's wife, was a former prostitute. His position became untenable and his natural replacement as head of the **Wehrmacht** was von Fritsch. However, Hitler disliked von Fritsch's views on military tactics, so he dismissed von Fritsch on trumped-up charges of homosexuality and replaced him with Keitel.

▓ *TIP* This episode helps to explain Hitler's acquisition of supreme political and military power in Germany.

Boer War, 1899–1902: a conflict (known also as the South African War) between the British empire and the two Dutch-speaking (Boer) republics of Transvaal and Orange Free State.

● The war was basically caused by the British desire to control southern Africa and to acquire gold deposits in the Transvaal.

● It took Britain 3 years to win the war, because the Boers used guerrilla tactics. The British retaliated by creating concentration camps for Boer women and children.

▓ *TIP* This war was the most serious armed conflict in the European partition of Africa. A lack of fit volunteers for the British Army led directly to the introduction of Liberal welfare reforms after 1906.

Bolshevik: a Russian communist. The term was first used to describe the faction of the Russian Social Democrat Party that supported *Lenin* in a split with the *Mensheviks* in 1903.

● Both Bolsheviks and Mensheviks believed in creating a socialist system in Russia. They differed on the tactics to achieve it. The Mensheviks wanted membership of the Social Democrat Party to be open to anyone who agreed with its aims. The Bolsheviks, under Lenin, wanted party membership restricted to full-time revolutionaries.

● The Bolsheviks became a separate party in 1912.

● Winning power in the *October Revolution of 1917*, the Bolshevik Party changed its name to the Communist Party in 1918.

▓ *TIP* The Bolshevik Party organisation was Lenin's major contribution to the development of communism. *Marx*'s ideas, combined with Lenin's organisational changes, created the concept of Marxist–Leninism.

Bonhoeffer, Dietrich: a Protestant pastor who was a vehement opponent of the Nazi regime in Germany.

● He signed the Barmen declaration in 1934, which opposed the Nazification of the Protestant Church.

● At the beginning of the Second World War he became involved in a conspiracy against *Hitler* and in 1942 went to Stockholm (capital of neutral Sweden) to try to mediate an end to the war with the Allies.

● He was arrested and imprisoned in a concentration camp by the *Gestapo* in 1943 and murdered by the *SS* in 1945.

▓ *TIP* Bonhoeffer was a shining example of principled opposition to the Hitler regime.

Bormann, Martin: a leading figure in the Nazi regime, becoming *Hitler*'s private secretary and head of the Reich Chancellery.

- As assistant to the Deputy Führer, Rudolf *Hess*, his power increased after Hess flew to Britain in 1941 on a peace mission. He was appointed head of the Chancellery thereafter.
- Widely regarded as one of the most influential figures in the Nazi regime during the Second World War, he dominated the Third Reich along with *Goering*, *Goebbels* and *Himmler*. Attempts to meet Hitler were usually successful only with Bormann's approval.

■ *TIP* A study of Bormann helps to explain how political power was distributed in the Nazi state below Hitler.

Borodino, Battle of, 1812: a Napoleonic victory. The battle took place outside Moscow during *Napoleon*'s invasion of Russia.

- Although Napoleon captured Moscow, the Russians set fire to the city as they retreated. He was left with an empty shell.
- Lack of supplies forced Napoleon into retreat through the winter of 1812–13. The cold and starvation led to mass desertions from his **Grande Armée**.

■ *TIP* This was the beginning of the eventual defeat of Napoleon.

Bosnian Crisis, 1908–09: precipitated when Austria-Hungary annexed the Turkish provinces of Bosnia and Herzegovina.

- Austria-Hungary had occupied the two provinces since the Treaty of *Berlin* in 1878. Russia and Serbia both opposed the annexation.
- In 1909 Russia threatened war against Austria-Hungary but was warned off by Germany, which supported Austria-Hungary.
- This was a dress rehearsal for the *July Crisis* of 1914.

■ *TIP* It is important to know what caused the crisis, and its impact on international relations, rather than what actually took place during the crisis.

Boulanger Affair, 1885–89: General Boulanger, French Minister of War in 1885, supported the campaign for the return of Alsace and Lorraine to France. This episode led to a major deterioration in Franco–German relations.

- Boulanger also threatened the Third French Republic by standing for election in a number of constituencies, each time successfully.
- To many French people he appeared to have the resolve needed to lead France back to a position of international strength.
- Opponents of Boulanger formed the Society of the Rights of Man. In 1889 the government attempted to arrest him, but he fled to Brussels and committed suicide.

■ *TIP* This affair, along with the *Panama Scandal* and the *Dreyfus* Affair, undermined support for the Third French Republic. However, in each case French democracy survived.

Brandt, Willy: West German Chancellor (1969–74), who won the Nobel Peace Prize in 1971 for his *Ostpolitik*, which brought closer relations between East and West Germany. He was also Mayor of West Berlin (1957–61).

b

- In 1980 he produced the Brandt Report for the UN on the world economy. It advocated a major redistribution of economic wealth from rich to poor countries.
- ■ *TIP* *Ostpolitik* was an important attempt to break down tensions between East and West in central Europe during the *Cold War*.

Brest-Litovsk, Treaty of, 1918: ended the First World War on the Eastern Front.
- The treaty was signed in March between Germany with Austria-Hungary and communist Russia.
- Russia was forced to give up the Baltic states of Latvia, Lithuania, Estonia and the Ukraine.
- As a result, Russia lost much of its industrial production and its most valuable agricultural land.
- The treaty led to a great debate in the Russian Communist Party, following which the left-wing *Social Revolutionaries* left the Russian government. They attempted to overthrow the communists and also made an unsuccessful assassination attempt on Lenin.
- The treaty allowed the Germans to concentrate all their armed forces on the Western Front, in a bid to win the war in the *March Offensive* of 1918.
- ■ *TIP* Brest-Litovsk revealed Germany's war aims in the East. They foreshadowed what *Hitler* tried to achieve in the Second World War.

Bretton Woods Agreement, 1944: a meeting of Allied powers, held in the USA, to decide on the organisation of international trade after the Second World War.
- They agreed on a policy of international exchange rates, where each currency would have a fixed value against the dollar. Any change in value could occur only through agreement.
- It also established the General Agreement on Tariffs and Trade (now known as the World Trade Organisation or WTO) to encourage free trade.
- It created the International Monetary Fund (IMF) to aid countries in financial difficulties, and the World Bank to lend money to poorer countries.
- ■ *TIP* The agreement provided the basis for postwar prosperity.

Brezhnev, Leonid: ruler of the *USSR* (1964–82) who, initially sharing power with Andrei Kosygin (until 1967), considerably enlarged the armed forces, particularly the Navy, and from 1971 began to improve relations with the USA in a policy of *détente*.
- Initially, *détente* involved cultural exchanges, such as those made by sports teams, but it also led to the *Strategic Arms Limitation Treaties* (SALT) of 1972 and 1979, which aimed to limit the number of nuclear weapons held by both the USSR and the USA.
- Better relations with the USA did not prevent the Soviet invasion and occupation of *Afghanistan* in 1979.
- In spite of Brezhnev's successes in foreign affairs, the Soviet economy was increasingly unable to support the government's military requirements. This led to economic stagnation in the 1980s.

■ *TIP* Brezhnev is an important figure in the *Cold War* and in the story of the eventual collapse of the USSR.

Brezhnev Doctrine, 1968: stated that a communist state had the right to intervene in the affairs of another communist state, if the political and economic system in that state was under threat.

● The doctrine was invoked in August 1968 to justify the Warsaw Pact invasion and occupation of Czechoslovakia (*Prague Spring*). It was also used to support the Soviet invasion of *Afghanistan* in December 1979.

■ *TIP* Use this term to explain Soviet policy towards other communist countries from 1968 onwards.

Britain, Battle of, 1940: the air battle which took place over southern England between June and October 1940, between the Royal Air Force and the German Luftwaffe. The British victory prevented a German invasion of Britain.

Brown v. Board of Education Case, 1954: a US *Supreme Court* case which ordered the racial desegregation of public schools.

● The order reversed the 1896 judgement in Plessy v. Ferguson, which had established the principle of separate but equal educational facilities.

● It declared that Plessy v. Ferguson denied African Americans equal protection under the law, guaranteed by the Fourteenth Amendment to the American Constitution.

● In 1955 it was followed by the Brown (II) case, which demanded that public schools be desegregated with 'all deliberate speed'.

● The decision met with strong resistance from state governments in the 'Old South'.

■ *TIP* The Brown case is central to any discussion of the *civil rights* movement from 1954 onwards. It provided strong constitutional support for the demands for civil and political equality made by African Americans.

Brüning, Heinrich: Chancellor of Germany (1930–32) who, faced with problems of mass unemployment and the collapse of the banking system, attempted to reduce government spending by cutting unemployment pay.

● As leader of the Catholic Centre Party, he was appointed by *Hindenburg* using Article 48 of the Constitution.

● He failed in his attempt to stop reparations payments, which Germany was forced to make as a result of its defeat in the First World War.

● His policies caused great resentment and he was dismissed by President Hindenburg and replaced by von Papen.

■ *TIP* The failure of Brüning's policies was an important factor in the rise in popularity of both the Nazi and Communist parties after 1930.

Brusilov Offensive, 1916: a Russian attack on the Eastern Front.

● Its initial success brought Romania into the First World War on the side of the Allies. However, it eventually failed to drive back the German and Austro-Hungarian armies.

● The offensive was the last success the Russians had in the First World War.

b

It served a purpose in diverting German troops away from the battles of *Verdun* and the *Somme* on the Western Front.

■ *TIP* The ultimate failure of the Brusilov Offensive led to desertions from the Russian Army and laid a foundation for the *February Revolution* against the Tsar early the following year.

Bukharin, Nikolai: a leading Russian communist, member of the *Politburo*, and editor of **Pravda**, the Soviet daily newspaper.

● He supported the *New Economic Policy* (NEP) in the late 1920s.

● However, he lost influence when *Stalin* changed tack, to support rapid industrialisation after 1928. Eventually he was put on trial and executed in the *Purges* of the mid-1930s.

■ *TIP* Bukharin represented the moderate wing of the Communist Party. Stalin supported him in his defeat of *Trotsky*, *Zinoviev* and *Kamenev*, in 1926–27, but then changed his views to defeat Bukharin and his supporters in 1928–29.

Bulgarian Crisis, 1885–87: an international crisis brought on by the political union of Bulgaria with eastern Roumelia.

● The crisis led to a brief war between Serbia and Bulgaria in 1886.

● Its main significance was for the conflict between Russia and Austria-Hungary. Russia opposed the union; Austria-Hungary supported it. This led to the collapse of the *Three Emperors Alliance* in 1887. Germany replaced it with the *Reinsurance Treaty* with Russia.

■ *TIP* The crisis brought to an end the period of international cooperation between Russia and Austria-Hungary. It also saw the beginning of the end of *Bismarck*'s system of alliances.

Burgfriede, 1914: a 'political truce' created in Germany at the beginning of the First World War, when all German political parties in the *Reichstag* (lower house of the national parliament) agreed to support the government. It included the socialist *Social Democrat Party* (SPD).

● The truce lasted until 1917, when a peace resolution was introduced into the Reichstag, calling on the government to negotiate an end to the war. Failure of the resolution led to a split in the SPD, with Independent Social Democrats (USPD) opposing the government's continued support for the war.

■ *TIP* *Burgfriede* is important in explaining how popular support for the war in 1914 led to growing opposition by 1917 — and, ultimately, to the German Revolution of October/November 1918.

Bush, George: US President (1989–93), who successfully led the Allied powers against Iraq in the *Gulf War* of 1991.

● He was also in power when communist control in eastern Europe collapsed in 1989, and then in the *USSR* in 1991. He succeeded Ronald *Reagan* and lost the 1992 presidential election to Bill *Clinton*.

Cadets: see *Kadets*.

Campo Formio Treaty, 1797: signed between Revolutionary France and Austria, following *Napoleon*'s successful Italian campaign of 1796–97.

- The treaty recognised the River Rhine as France's eastern frontier. It also recognised the loss of the Austrian Netherlands (Belgium) to France.
- In Italy, it recognised the end of Venetian independence and the creation of the Cisalpine Republic in north Italy.

■ *TIP* The treaty was a triumph for Napoleon. It established him as hero of the *Directory* and laid the foundations for his assumption of power in 1800.

Canning, George: British Foreign Secretary (1822–27), who was opposed to the *Congress System*.

- He particularly disliked *Metternich*, the Austrian Chancellor.
- He supported the independence of Spain's Latin American colonies and the Greek desire for independence from the *Ottoman* (Turkish) *empire*. In 1825–27 he worked with France and Russia to help the Greeks. This cooperation led to the Battle of Navarino Bay in 1827, where the combined fleets of Britain, France and Russia defeated the Turks.
- His early death in 1827 prevented him from stopping the Russo–Turkish War of 1828–29.

■ *TIP* Canning opposed the Congress System, but was a keen supporter of the *Concert of Europe*. Many of his views on foreign policy were followed by *Palmerston* between 1830 and 1865.

Carbonari: an Italian secret society which wished to create liberal regimes. It operated in the 1820s and is associated with the revolutions of 1820–21.

Carlsbad Decrees, 1819: anti-liberal measures passed by the diet (assembly) of the *German Confederation*.

- They were introduced following the assassination of Kotzebue and were designed to suppress student organisations (***Burschenschaften)***, censor the press and establish a committee in Mainz to investigate liberal organisations within the confederation.

■ *TIP* The decrees were a triumph for *Metternich* and are a good example of how he attempted to limit the spread of liberal ideas after 1815.

Carter, Jimmy: US President (1977–81), whose major triumph was the Camp David agreement of 1978 between Egypt under *Sadat* and Israel under Begin, which brought to an end the war between these two states and the return of Sinai to Egypt.

- Carter also negotiated the *SALT* II treaty, but this was rejected by the US Senate following the Soviet invasion of *Afghanistan* in 1979.
- Carter's biggest foreign policy problem was the Iranian Revolution of 1979. The Shah was overthrown by an Islamic fundamentalist government under Ayatollah *Khomeini*. Iranian hostility to America resulted in the US embassy hostage crisis of 1979–81.
- Carter's failures over Afghanistan and Iran were important factors in his electoral defeat by Ronald *Reagan* in 1980.

Castro, Fidel: Cuban revolutionary and Marxist ruler of the Caribbean island since 1959.

- With his brother Raul and Che Guevara, he led the 26 July Revolutionary Movement, which overthrew the Batista dictatorship in 1959.
- He created a socialist state and developed strong links with the *USSR*.
- The *CIA*-sponsored invasion by Cuban exiles at the *Bay of Pigs* fiasco of April 1961 was defeated by Castro's forces. He faced repeated US attempts to assassinate him.
- He invited the USSR to place nuclear missiles and military personnel on Cuba in 1962, which resulted in the *Cuban Missile Crisis* in October of that year.
- He also sponsored left-wing *guerrilla* movements in Latin America, but without success. In the 1970s he sent troops to Africa to assist Angola in the war with UNITA and South Africa, and to the Ethiopian regime of Mengistu.

■ TIP Castro is a wily Marxist revolutionary leader, established close to America, who has survived over 40 years of US opposition to stay in power.

Cavour, Count Camillo di: Prime Minister of Piedmont-Sardinia (1849–61), who was instrumental in the formation of the Kingdom of Italy.

- His main foreign policy aim was to make Piedmont-Sardinia the dominant north Italian state.
- He gained the support of France, in the Pact of *Plombières* (1858), as a way of achieving this aim. The Franco–Austrian war of 1860 led to the acquisition of Lombardy by Piedmont-Sardinia.
- Cavour's greatest triumph came in 1860–61, when he persuaded the populations of Parma, Modena, Tuscany and the Papal State of the Romagna to join Piedmont-Sardinia.
- He also persuaded King Victor Emmanuel II of Piedmont-Sardinia to invade the Papal States, in the summer of 1860.
- He helped to negotiate the creation of the Kingdom of Italy in 1861, with the inclusion of the Kingdom of Naples and Sicily, which had been conquered by *Garibaldi* in 1860.

■ TIP Remember, Cavour's original aim was to make Piedmont-Sardinia the dominant north Italian state. He didn't want to unify Italy. Cavour used the rapid change of events in the 1860s to Piedmont-Sardinia's advantage — which resulted in the creation of the Kingdom of Italy.

Ceauşescu, Nicolae: communist ruler of Romania, 1965–89.

- He developed an independent line in foreign policy, separate from the *USSR*. He signed trade agreements with both the USA and West European states, most notably France.
- Domestically, he operated a harsh dictatorship. Secret police dealt severely with all political opposition.
- In 1989, with the fall of communist regimes across eastern Europe, he was overthrown in a bloody uprising and killed.

▨ *TIP* He was a major political leader in eastern Europe from the 1960s to the 1980s, whose liberal foreign policy stood in marked contrast to his repressive rule at home.

cede (vb)**:** to give up territory to another state. For instance, Czechoslovakia ceded the *Sudetenland* to Germany as part of the *Munich* Agreement of September 1938.

CENTO: see *Central Treaty Organisation*.

Central Intelligence Agency (CIA): the primary intelligence and foreign affairs agency of the USA, created by the National Security Act, 1947.

- It has been used extensively by presidents for covert foreign operations. *Eisenhower* used the CIA to help overthrow the Arbenz regime in Guatemala and the Mossadeq regime in Iran. *Kennedy* used the CIA to organise a war against the Pathet Lao communist army in Laos in 1961.
- In the *Vietnam War* it ran the *Phoenix Programme* of political assassination against known communists. Under *Nixon* the CIA was used to overthrow the Allende regime in Chile in 1973. *Reagan* used the agency to organise Contra guerrillas in Nicaragua in the 1980s.

▨ *TIP* It can be viewed as part of the growth of the 'imperial presidency' — a secretive organisation used to further US interests abroad, often without Congressional knowledge or approval.

Central Treaty Organisation (CENTO), 1959: a military organisation which, along with *NATO* and *SEATO*, was used to support the USA and the West in the *Cold War*.

- CENTO originated with the British-sponsored Baghdad Pact of 1955.
- It was used to contain Iraq, Turkey, Iran and Pakistan.
- It came to an end in the late 1970s, with the *Iranian Revolution*.

▨ *TIP* Use the term when covering *Eisenhower*'s policy towards the *USSR*. The USA sought to create political/military alliances around the USSR. This became part of the *New Look foreign policy* of the Republican administration.

Centre Party: a Catholic party in Germany, active from 1870 to 1933.

- It first gained popular support in defence of Catholic rights during *Bismarck*'s *Kulturkampf* of 1872–85.

- Its main support came from western and southern Germany and at its height it gained some 90 seats in the *Reichstag*.
- The party eventually voted itself out of existence in 1933, in return for a *concordat* between *Hitler*'s government and the Pope.

Chamberlain, Neville: British Prime Minister (1937–40), who was closely associated with the policy of *appeasement*.

- He helped negotiate the *Munich* Agreement of September 1938 with *Hitler* over the *Sudetenland* of Czechoslovakia.
- Much criticised for his actions following the Second World War, Chamberlain had little choice but to espouse the policy of appeasement in 1938, because Britain was militarily unprepared for war and the British public, and public opinion in the Commonwealth, did not support war with Germany at that time.
- He abandoned appeasement following the German take-over of Bohemia and Moravia in 1939.
- He resigned as Prime Minister following the German conquest of Denmark and Norway.

▨ *TIP* Chamberlain is a central figure in any debate on the causes of the Second World War in Europe. Historians are divided on whether the Munich Agreement was a triumph for Hitler or for Chamberlain.

Charles X: King of France (1824–30), the last French king from the Bourbon family, who was overthrown by the *July Revolution*.

- Seen as a very conservative king, he wanted to undermine the Constitution (*Charter*) of 1814–15.
- He issued the *Ordinances of St Cloud* in 1830, which attempted to undermine the authority of the French national parliament.
- This led to the 'three glorious days' at the end of July, when the Paris mob took control of the capital and declared *Louis Philippe* of the Orleans family the 'Citizen King'.

▨ *TIP* Charles X's personal actions were a major cause of the fall of the Bourbon Restoration.

Charles Albert: King of Piedmont-Sardinia (1831–49), a conservative ruler who became a liberal reformer.

- He introduced the *Statuto*, a liberal constitution, just before he abdicated in favour of his son, Victor Emanuel II, in March 1849.
- Charles Albert's resignation took place following Piedmont-Sardinia's heavy military defeat by Austria, at the Battle of Novara.

▨ *TIP* Charles Albert established Piedmont-Sardinia as Italy's most liberal state and a major opponent of Austrian influence.

Charter: the Constitution of France, 1814–48.

- The Charter created a constitutional monarchy in France, where political power was shared between the monarch and a national parliament.
- The Charter was undermined by *Charles X*, who wanted more political power. This led to his overthrow in the *July Revolution*. From 1830 to 1848 the Charter

became a national constitution, following the election of *Louis Philippe* as a citizen king.

■ *TIP* Knowing the terms of the Charter is an important start to the study of France in this period.

Cheka (All-Russia Extraordinary Commission): a communist secret police force created by Lenin in 1918.

● Under the leadership of Felix Dzerzhinsky, the Cheka organised acts of political terror against opponents of the communist government.

● It was a forerunner of subsequent Soviet terror police forces, the *OGPU* and the *NKVD*.

Chernenko, Konstantin: Soviet leader (1984–85), who kept *Gorbachev* waiting for power.

● The *Politburo* chose the ageing and conservative Chernenko ahead of Yuri *Andropov*'s chosen successor, the younger and reformist Mikhail Gorbachev. Many of the elderly Politburo members feared that Gorbachev would remove them if he was given power.

● Already very ill when he became leader, Chernenko survived a mere 13 months before power was eventually handed to Gorbachev on his death.

■ *TIP* He was the last truly conservative leader of the *USSR*.

Chiang Kai Shek: a Chinese nationalist general and leader of the *Kuomintang* (Nationalist) Party.

● He fought against the Chinese communists from 1927 until his defeat in the Civil War in 1949.

● During the Second World War he took part in *Great Power* negotiations with Britain and the USA in Cairo in 1943.

● Following his defeat in 1949, he founded Nationalist China on the island of Taiwan (formerly Formosa).

■ *TIP* Chiang was an important ally of the USA from the 1930s up to 1949. The loss of China to communism in 1949 undermined President *Truman*'s administration in the USA.

Churchill, Winston: British Prime Minister, 1940–45 and 1951–55.

● Britain's wartime leader took office shortly before the German *blitzkrieg* on the West began.

● He refused to accept the proposal of negotiating with *Hitler*, following the fall of France in 1940, urging Britain to fight on alone until June 1941, when the *USSR* entered the war.

● He formed a close relationship with US President Franklin D. *Roosevelt* in 1940–41, which led to *lend-lease* and the *Atlantic Charter*.

● He was a member of the 'Big Three' of the Grand Alliance, along with Roosevelt and *Stalin*, and attended the *Tehran*, *Yalta* and first *Potsdam* conferences. Fearing that the postwar world would be dominated by the USA and the USSR, he attempted to split the other two powers apart, helping to create the *Cold War* after 1945.

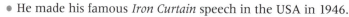

C

- He made his famous *Iron Curtain* speech in the USA in 1946.
- He led the Conservative Party to defeat in 1945 and 1950, but to victory in 1951.
- **■ *TIP*** Churchill's powers of leadership were a major factor in Britain's war effort in the Second World War.

CIA: see *Central Intelligence Agency.*

Civil Constitution of the Clergy, 1790: a controversial edict passed by the National Assembly, bringing the French Catholic Church under political control.
- Priests and other religious personnel received salaries from the government and had to swear an oath of loyalty to the state.
- The edict was reluctantly accepted by *Louis XVI* in August, but was never accepted by the Pope.
- It remained in force under the *concordat* between *Napoleon* and the Pope in 1801.
- **■ *TIP*** This edict constituted a major part of the revolutionary change brought about in France, 1789–90. It must be seen alongside the *Constitution of 1791.*

Civilian Conservation Corps, 1933: a corps of young men recruited by the US Department of Labor in an attempt to reduce unemployment during the first *New Deal.*
- Males between 17 and 24 were organised on military lines to work on re-forestation, soil conservation and improvement in the National Parks for 9 months each.
- Initially established for 2 years, the scheme was extended in 1935 for a further 7 years.
- **■ *TIP*** Establishment of the corps was an important ingredient of the first 100 days, which aimed to offer relief to the unemployed.

Civil Rights Acts: acts passed by *Congress* (the national parliament of the USA) to give political and civil rights to African Americans and other minority groups.
- The first act was passed in 1875 and was followed by others in 1957 and 1960.
- Most important was the 1964 Act, passed during the *Johnson* administration. It guaranteed federal support for political and civil equality for minority groups. Article VII of the act guaranteed equality for women.
- **■ *TIP*** The 1957 and 1960 acts had limited impact, because they contained weak enforcement powers. The 1964 Act should be seen as one of the major landmarks in the creation of civil equality in the USA.

Civil Works Administration, 1933: this was created to offer emergency relief to the unemployed during the winter of 1933–34, during the first *New Deal.*
- It received $400 million which had been given to the *Public Works Administration.*
- It was closed down in March 1934, having provided work for 4 million unemployed people.
- **■ *TIP*** This was an emergency measure set up to meet difficulties created for poor people by the harsh winter.

Clemenceau, Georges: a French statesman who led France to victory in the First World War. He was Prime Minister, 1906–09 and 1917–20.

- He helped to finalise the separation of Church from state in 1906–09.
- During the First World War he secured the appointment of Ferdinand Foch as Commander of all Allied forces on the Western Front in 1918.
- At the *Paris* Peace Conference Clemenceau wanted to destroy Germany's ability to wage war. He advocated the creation of a Rhineland republic and was a major force behind the creation of the demilitarised Rhineland and the reduction in German armed forces. He came into conflict with US President *Wilson*, who wanted what he believed to be a more just and balanced peace.
- *TIP* He was an important Allied statesman, who played a major part in the Paris peace settlement. He was one of the 'Big Three', along with *Lloyd George* of Britain and Woodrow Wilson of the USA.

Clinton, Bill: US President (1993–2001), whose presidency was characterised by economic prosperity and domestic scandal.

- In his second term (1997–2001), Clinton, a Democrat, was affected by the 'Monica Lewinsky affair', which led to his impeachment by a Republican-controlled *Congress*. The impeachment failed, due to the lack of a two-thirds majority in the Senate.
- In foreign affairs, the USA became involved in the Bosnian Civil War and also attacked Iraq in Operation Desert Fox, because of unacceptable treatment of *United Nations* weapons inspectors. The USA also became involved in the Kosovo War of 1999, as part of *NATO*.
- *TIP* He was the first president to conduct foreign policy completely in a post-*Cold War* setting.

Coalitions against the French Revolution and Napoleon: the group of states which fought against France, 1792–1815.

- The First Coalition of countries was formed in 1792 and included Austria, Prussia, Britain, Spain, Portugal, Naples and Holland. This came to an end with the withdrawal of Prussia.
- The Second Coalition lasted from 1799 to 1802 and contained Britain, Austria, Russia, Naples and Portugal. It came to an end in 1801–02, after French victories at Marengo and Hohenlinden.
- The Third Coalition contained Austria, Prussia, Russia, Sweden and Britain. It lasted from 1804 to 1807. It came to an end after *Napoleon*'s victories at Austerlitz (1805) and Jena (1806).
- The Fourth Coalition lasted from 1812 until Napoleon's eventual defeat in 1815. It contained Britain, Austria, Prussia, Russia and Sweden. The coalition won major victories at Leipzig (1813) and *Waterloo* (1815).
- *TIP* Coalitions were the major diplomatic response to the French Revolution by other European countries.

Cold War: a term used to describe international tension between the USA and its allies and the *USSR* and its allies between 1945 and 1991.

C

- It did not involve a direct military confrontation between the superpowers, but it did involve wars between smaller allies on each sides, e.g. the *Korean War* (1950–53) and the *Vietnam War* (1946–73).
- The Cold War was largely a propaganda war between the competing ideologies of communism and capitalism.
- It also involved a major military build-up, where both sides were in constant readiness for war. A principal feature was the maintenance of large nuclear forces.
- The Cold War came to an end when the USSR failed to match US military spending. This failure undermined the Soviet economy, and with it Soviet control of eastern Europe.
- ▩ *TIP* The Cold War has been the chief feature of European and international relations since 1945. The vast majority of international conflicts since the Second World War can be seen to have a Cold War dimension.

collectivisation (of Soviet agriculture)**:** the taking over of private farm holdings by the state, to be turned into large agricultural units known as either a *kolkhoz* (collective farm owned by the workers) or a *sovkhoz* (collective farm owned directly by the government). This was part of *Stalin*'s plan to modernise the Soviet economy after 1928.

- The policy of forced collectivisation met with considerable peasant resistance. By 1932–33 it had resulted in a famine in the Ukraine, causing approximately 4–5 million deaths.
- It also destroyed the Soviet peasantry as a separate economic class.
- ▩ *TIP* Collectivisation was central to economic planning during Stalin's rule. It caused his greatest economic failure and led to major criticism of him in the Communist Party. His reply to this criticism was to begin the *Purges*.

Comecon (Council for Mutual Economic Assistance)**:** set up by the *USSR* in 1949 as a communist equivalent of *Marshall Aid*.

- It promoted economic cooperation between the USSR and its east European satellite states.
- It lasted until the collapse of communism in eastern Europe in 1989.
- ▩ *TIP* Comecon was an economic, not a political, organisation; so don't confuse it with *Cominform*.

Cominform (Communist Information Bureau)**:** created by the *USSR* in 1947 to help coordinate the activities of European communist parties.

- Yugoslavia was expelled from Cominform in 1948, because the Yugoslav leader, *Tito*, refused to follow the Soviet leadership.
- It came to an end after the denunciation of *Stalin* by *Khrushchev*, at the Twentieth Congress of the Soviet Communist Party in 1956.

Comintern (Communist International)**:** set up by *Lenin* in 1919 to coordinate the activities of communist parties around the world. It was his attempt to spread communist world revolution.

- Its first leader was Grigory *Zinoviev*.

- It failed to spread communism beyond the borders of the *USSR*. Comintern gave the German Communist Party instructions to concentrate its opposition on the Social Democrats, rather than the Nazis. The resulting split between the two left-wing parties helped *Hitler* to gain power.
- From 1934 onwards, communist parties across Europe were instructed to join with socialists against right-wing groups. This led to the formation of so-called 'popular front' governments in France (1935) and Spain (1936).
- The Comintern was abolished by *Stalin* during the Second World War.
- **TIP** Do not confuse the three terms listed above. The Comintern was associated with the interwar years. Comecon and Cominform belong in the Cold War period.

commissar: a Russian communist term for government minister.

- After the *Bolshevik* Revolution of 1917 Lenin created the first communist government, known as the Council of People's Commissars.
- In that first government *Trotsky* was Commissar for Foreign Affairs and *Stalin* Commissar for Nationalities.
- In Operation *Barbarossa*, the German High Command was issued with instructions from *Hitler* to put to death all Soviet commissars; in this context Hitler meant all Communist Party officials.
- **TIP** Make sure you use this term, instead of 'minister', when writing about Communist Russia in the period 1917–45.

Committee of Public Safety: set up in March 1793 by the Revolutionary *Convention* in France. Its original aim was to recruit soldiers, but under *Robespierre* it became organiser of the *Terror*. It used Revolutionary committees to maintain control in the provinces.

- Its power came to an end in July 1794, with the fall of Robespierre during the *Thermidorian Reaction.*
- **TIP** The Committee is central to any study of the French Revolutionary Terror. Remember, during the 1792–94 phase of the Revolution, several committees were created. For instance, the Committee of General Defence existed at the same time. It had authority over the police, but was subordinate to the Committee of Public Safety.

Committee of Twelve: a French Revolutionary committee set up by the *Girondins* in May 1793 to attack their enemies, the more extreme radicals the *Hebertists.*

- It came to an end with the fall of the Girondins in June 1793, when the Commander of the National Guard forced ten of the twelve committee members to resign.
- **TIP** Be aware that, during the French Revolution, different types of committee were created by the *Convention.*

Common Agricultural Policy: a major, but controversial, policy of the European Union (EU), introduced in 1964, which subsidises agricultural production in EU countries. It comprises over 80% of the EU budget.

- The policy has been blamed for sustaining inefficient farming methods.

C

Commune: the government of Paris during the French Revolution.

- During 1792–94 it was controlled by the *sans culottes*.
- In August 1792 the Commune forced the National Assembly to arrest 'enemies of the state'. This action led directly to the creation of the *First Republic* in September 1792 and the creation of the *Convention.*

Commune of 1871: set up during the civil war which followed the French defeat in the Franco–Prussian War of 1870–71, when opponents of the government of Adolphe *Thiers* established self-governing communes, most notably in Paris, but also in other towns.

- Members of the communes (communards) were idealistic radicals, who supported socialist and democratic ideas.
- They were suppressed with great severity by government troops.
- The Paris Commune marked the last great uprising of the metropolitan population.
- ▌*TIP* The Commune was one of the most important consequences of the fall of the Second Empire (1852–70). Its suppression left a lasting impact on the history of the Third French Republic (1870–1940). It should be mentioned when discussing the weaknesses of the Third Republic.

Concert of Europe: a term used in international relations between 1815 and 1914, based on the belief that the *balance of power* in Europe could be maintained only when the *Great Powers* acted together, in concert.

- The concept was utilised to solve crises associated with Greek independence (1827–32), the *Belgian Revolt* (1830–39), *Mehemet Ali* (1841) and the *Great Eastern Crisis* (1878).
- ▌*TIP* The *Congress System* of 1815–25 was one aspect of the Concert of Europe in action.

concordat: an agreement between the Pope and a national government.

- In 1801 *Napoleon* signed a concordat with the Pope. It recognised Catholicism as the religion of the majority of French people. In return, the Pope recognised Napoleon's regime.
- In 1933 *Hitler* signed a concordat. He guaranteed independence for the Catholic Church in Germany. In return, the Catholic *Centre Party* dissolved itself, paving the way for the creation of a one-party Nazi state.
- ▌*TIP* Remember that the term refers to the Pope in the Vatican. Up until 1870, and then from 1929 onwards, the Pope has been the monarch of an independent state, the Vatican City. Therefore, a concordat is effectively an agreement between two countries.

Confederation of the Rhine, 1806: an organisation of German states established by *Napoleon* to replace the Holy Roman Empire.

- Napoleon was declared Protector of the Confederation. Austria and Prussia were excluded.
- *Serfdom* and other feudal privileges were abolished.
- The Confederation was an ally of France until Napoleon's defeat in 1814.

■ *TIP* The Confederation should be mentioned when explaining how Napoleon reorganised Europe between 1805 and 1815.

Congress: the national parliament of the United States, divided into two houses, the Senate and the House of Representatives.

- The Senate contains two representatives per state, each elected for 6 years. Since 1913, senators have been directly elected.
- The House of Representatives contains 435 members, each elected for 2 years. The number of House seats allocated per state is based on the density of population.
- The Senate has the power of 'advice and consent' over government appointments and foreign treaties.
- The House's main responsibility is for finance.
- Both houses must agree if a bill is to become an act (become law). US acts usually carry the name of the Senate and House sponsors, e.g. the *Wagner–Connery Act*, 1935.

■ *TIP* A knowledge of the role and responsibilities of Congress is essential to an understanding of US history.

Congress System: a series of international meetings by the *Great Powers* following the defeat of *Napoleon*. They took place at *Aix-la-Chapelle* in 1818, *Troppau* in 1820, *Laibach* in 1821 and *Verona* in 1822.

- Article VI of the Second Treaty of Paris (1815) suggested that the Great Powers should meet from time to time to discuss the affairs of Europe.
- However, differences between the Great Powers soon emerged. In 1815 Britain refused to join the *Holy Alliance*. In 1820 Britain refused to sign the Troppau Protocol, which gave the Great Powers authority to intervene anywhere that there was an outbreak of liberal revolution.
- Although the Congress System had come to an end by the mid-1820s, the idea of Great Power cooperation continued through the operation of the *Concert of Europe*.

■ *TIP* The Congress System is of central importance in any study of European international relations following the defeat of Napoleon. Terms such as *balance of power* and Concert of Europe are important in understanding the Congress System.

conscription: compulsory military service.

- First introduced by Carnot during the French Revolution, conscription led to the creation of large armies.
- By 1870 all *Great Powers*, except Britain, had introduced conscription. When war was imminent, trained civilians could be called up quickly for military service.
- This process of mobilisation was of great importance in forcing politicians to make quick decisions during the *July Crisis* of 1914.

■ *TIP* Introduce the concept when explaining the changing nature of warfare since the 1790s.

Constitution of 1791 (France): the work of the Constituent Assembly, it created a constitutional (as opposed to an absolute) monarchy.

- The king was declared 'King of the French by the grace of God and the will of the nation'. The monarch's private estates became public property. The king was head of government (the executive), but had no power over the legislature.
- The legislature was to consist of a single chamber with 745 members, to sit for 2 years only. Legislation could be suspended by the king's veto.
- The legislature was to be elected by 'active citizens' (men over 25 who paid direct taxes).
- In local government, France was divided into 83 departments, subdivided into 374 cantons, divided into 44,000 communes.
- *TIP* This was an important political achievement of the National Assembly phase of the French Revolution.

Consulate: the system of government in Revolutionary France, from the fall of the Directory in 1799 to 1804, when *Napoleon* declared the First French Empire.

- Although there were three consuls, Napoleon, as First Consul, dominated the government.
- *TIP* The Consulate was an important phase in the establishment of Napoleon's dictatorship.

containment: the US policy introduced with the *Truman Doctrine* of March 1947, whose aim was to contain the spread of communist influence.

- The policy pursued during the *Berlin Airlift Crisis* of 1948–49 is an example of containment in Europe.
- President *Truman's* decision to fight the communists in the *Korean War* is an example of containment in Asia.
- Even though Truman's successor, *Eisenhower*, wanted to roll back communism around the world, in effect he continued the policy of containment.
- *TIP* The concept is essential if you are to discuss the deterioration in East–West relations after 1945.

Continental blockade: introduced by *Napoleon* with the *Berlin Decrees* of 1806, the blockade was intended to defeat Britain by preventing trade with French-occupied Europe.

- Britain retaliated with Orders in Council (1807) banning trade with neutrals who traded with French-occupied Europe.
- The Continental blockade failed, because most French-occupied states wanted to buy British manufactures.
- *TIP* Use the term along with the Berlin Decrees and Orders in Council. It is an important aspect of Franco–British relations during Napoleon's rule.

Convention, French Revolutionary: the legislature of France, 1792–95. Proposed by *Robespierre,* and created at the height of the economic crisis, the Convention replaced the Legislative Assembly and declared a Republic in September 1792. It tried and executed *Louis XVI* in January 1793.

- It also created the Committee of General Defence (January 1793), the

Revolutionary Tribunal (February 1793) and the *Committee of Public Safety* (April 1793).

- It instituted the *Terror*, but its influence was affected by growth in the power of the *Commune*.
- It fell in 1795 and was replaced by the *Directory*.
- **TIP** The Convention oversaw the worst excesses of the French Revolution, most notably the Terror. It was dominated by the *Jacobins*.

Coolidge, Calvin: US President (1923–29), who claimed that 'the business of America is business'.

- He succeeded Warren *Harding*, who died in office, and oversaw the economic prosperity of 1920s America.
- He supported laissez-faire economic policy, which involved minimal government interference in the economy.
- Although the USA experienced widespread prosperity, African Americans and farmers suffered during his presidency. He vetoed the McNary–Haugen bill twice, which sought to give federal support to farmers.
- **TIP** Coolidge's low-key style characterised the American government's approach to economic affairs in the 1920s.

corporate state: created by *Mussolini* in an attempt to end the conflict in Italy in the 1920s between capital (businessmen and landowners) and labour (trade unions), with 'corporations' for every industry and occupation, where employers and employees were both represented.

- Twenty-two corporations were created, which came under the direction of the Ministry of Corporations.
- In 1939 the national parliament was replaced by a Chamber of Fasces and Corporations.
- **TIP** Study of the corporate state is central to an understanding of *fascist* Italy.

Council of Europe: an organisation of democratic European states, established in May 1949.

- Its aim is to develop common links between member states.
- Its main achievement was the creation of the European Court of Human Rights.
- Since 1989 membership of the Council has been the first step for former communist east European states to integrate with western Europe.
- **TIP** Do not confuse the Council of Europe with the European Union. They are completely different organisations.

Coup of 18th Brumaire, 1799: a political take-over in France, which ended the *Directory* period.

- The coup was organised by Abbé Sieyes, Barras and *Napoleon*'s brother Lucien.
- It led to the creation of a new government of three (Napoleon, Sieyes and Ducos), the Triumvirate who would act as a provisional government in order to produce a new constitution.
- **TIP** The coup was an important event in the rise of Napoleon to the creation of a military dictatorship in France.

C

Crimean War, 1853–56: a war in eastern Europe involving Russia on one side against the *Ottoman empire* (Turkey), Britain, France and Piedmont-Sardinia on the other.

- Although they did not fight, Austria and Sweden joined the allies against Russia.
- This was the first *Great Power* European war since 1815. It was an episode in the *Eastern Question*, with Russia attempting to gain territory and influence in the Ottoman empire.
- Most of the fighting took place in the Crimean peninsula in southern Russia, where British and French forces besieged the Sebastopol naval base.
- When Sebastopol fell in 1855 Russia began peace negotiations, which ended with the Treaty of *Paris* (1856). Russia lost the right to keep a fleet in the Black Sea and lost southern Bessarabia to Turkey.
- ▪ *TIP* The Crimean War was an important event in Russian history. Following Russia's humiliating defeat on its own soil, the new Tsar, *Alexander II*, began major internal reform, which included emancipating the serfs. The Crimean War also saw the end of the *Holy Alliance*, when Russia and Austria ceased to be allies. Consequently, Russia did not become involved in the unification of either Italy or Germany.

Cuban Missile Crisis, 1962: the most serious crisis in the *Cold War*, caused by the *USSR* placing nuclear missiles on Cuba, within 100 miles of the US coast.

- President *Kennedy* considered invading Cuba, which could have started a third world war. Instead, on the advice of his brother Robert, he blockaded the island.
- The Soviet leader, *Khrushchev,* backed down and withdrew Soviet missiles, in return for the dismantling of US missile sites in Turkey.
- ▪ *TIP* Resolution of the crisis was Kennedy's greatest diplomatic triumph. It also led to a new phase of cooperation between the USA and USSR. In 1963 they signed a nuclear *Test Ban Treaty*. A direct telephone link between the White House and the Kremlin was also established.

Cultural Revolution, 1966–69: a period of political upheaval, when the Chinese communist leader, *Mao Zedong*, used young communists ('Red Guards') to attack and remove from office the old Communist Party establishment in China.

- Many leaders lost office and the Chinese Communist Revolution became more radical. Madame Mao (Mao's wife) became a leading figure.
- The Cultural Revolution enabled Mao to regain political power, which he kept until his death in 1977.
- ▪ *TIP* This was a key event in splitting Red China away from the *USSR*.

D'Annunzio, Gabriele: an Italian nationalist and war hero in the First World War, who opposed the peace settlement.

- As a result, in September 1919 he occupied the Adriatic port of Fiume, which had been given to the new state of Yugoslavia, with volunteer troops.
- He set up a government, which was later used as a model for *Mussolini's fascists*. D'Annunzio was forced to leave Fiume in January 1921 by the Italian Navy.
- **■ *TIP*** In exam questions on the rise of Mussolini, D'Annunzio's government in Fiume is important, both as an example to the fascists and as an episode which undermined liberal government in Italy.

Danton, Georges Jacques: a French Revolutionary politician, who voted for the execution of *Louis XVI* (1793) and was an original member of the *Committee of Public Safety*.

- He was President of the *Jacobin* Club, but became disillusioned with the *Terror* and ended up as an enemy of *Robespierre* and the Mountain.
- He was arrested, tried and executed (1794).
- His death led to the ascendency of Robespierre in the French government.
- **■ *TIP*** It is important to understand how and why Danton changed his political views between 1792 and 1794, as the French Revolution became more radical.

Dawes Plan, 1924: an international agreement on German *reparations*, whereby Germany received loans from the USA, which enabled it to pay reparations to the European Allies.

- Reparations payments were also altered, to be raised from taxation and to be made in gold.
- In 1929 German reparations were further revised by the *Young Plan*.
- **■ *TIP*** The Dawes Plan played an important part in the German economic recovery, following the severe crisis of 1922–24 associated with *hyperinflation*. It should be studied in conjunction with the work of Gustav *Stresemann* and the stabilisation of the German currency with the introduction of the *Rentenmark* in 1924.

D-Day, 6 June 1944: the day on which an amphibious invasion of German-occupied France by the USA, Britain and Canada began, as a prelude to the defeat of Germany in the West by ground forces.

- It involved over a year's planning and resulted in the opening of the Second Front which *Stalin*, the Soviet leader, required of the Western Allies.
- It took place at the same time as Operation *Bagration* by the *Red Army* on the Eastern Front.
- The invasion resulted in a German defeat in Normandy by August 1944, and the beginning of the last phase of the Second World War in Europe.
- **TIP** Exam questions will require an explanation of the significance of the D-Day landings, rather than details about what took place.

death camps: concentration camps created for the specific purpose of exterminating perceived enemies of Nazi Germany.

- The camps were set up following the *Wannsee Conference* (1942).
- Their initial aim was to exterminate the Jewish population of Poland, but this was later extended to all European Jews and gypsies.
- Death camps were established in German-occupied Poland at Auschwitz, Sobibor, Treblinka, Belzec and Maidanek. Each camp contained gas chambers and crematoria for the rapid murder and disposal of victims. However, camps such as Auschwitz also contained prisoners, who worked as slave labourers in German-owned industrial plants.
- **TIP** These were the primary instruments of the Nazi policy known as the *Final Solution*. Of the 6 million Jews murdered, approximately 4 million died in death camps.

decolonisation: giving up control over imperial possessions.

- Between 1945 and the 1970s, European countries gave independence to their overseas possessions.
- In most cases this was achieved peacefully. In others it occurred as a result of war. For instance, the French in Indo-China and Algeria decolonised these areas only after long wars. Portugal gave up its African colonies in the 1970s following *guerrilla* wars.
- The first major decolonisation was the British withdrawal from the Indian subcontinent in 1947, with the creation of the independent states of India and Pakistan.
- Many problems arose in newly independent states, due to lack of a common language, culture or a strong political tradition. This often led to further conflict, e.g. in the former Belgian Congo and Nigeria.
- **TIP** Decolonisation is a central feature of the postwar foreign policies of Britain and France.

de Gaulle, Charles: French President (1959–69), who also led the Free French forces during the Second World War after the fall of France in 1940.

- He became President of a provisional government of France (1944–46), and again during the Algerian crisis in January 1959.
- He produced a new constitution, creating the Fifth French Republic, and gave independence to Algeria and other French colonies (1959–60).
- Developing an independent position in foreign affairs, he took France out of

NATO in 1964 and forged closer ties with the *USSR* and east European states.

● He was responsible for France twice vetoing British entry to the *European Economic Community (EEC)* (1963 and 1967).

● He resigned from office following the French 'revolution' of 1968 against his plans to reform the constitution.

■ TIP De Gaulle was a major figure in European *decolonisation* and the development of the EEC.

Deng Xiao Ping: leader of communist China (1977–98), who rose to political power following the death of *Mao Zedong*.

● He led moves to improve international relations with the West and the *USSR* and to increase Chinese economic and military power.

● He began the relaxation of government control of the economy.

● However, in 1989 he refused to accept calls for political reform, sending the army to crush student protests in *Tiananmen Square*.

■ TIP In the 1970s and 80s Deng was a central figure in explaining the improvement in international relations in Asia between East and West.

destalinisation: a policy designed to remove the more extreme aspects of political repression in the *USSR*.

● The policy was announced by the Soviet leader, *Khrushchev,* at the Twentieth Congress of the Soviet Communist Party in 1956. Khrushchev denounced the cult of personality.

● Thousands of political prisoners were released from the *Gulag* concentration camp system.

● A more liberal regime in the USSR led, in 1956, to attempts by Poland and Hungary to achieve greater independence. The *Hungarian Uprising* was ruthlessly crushed by the *Red Army*.

■ TIP Destalinisation was a major aspect of Khrushchev's domestic policy.

détente: an improvement in international relations, particularly between the USA and the *USSR* from 1971 onwards.

● The main architects of the policy were Richard *Nixon* of the USA and Leonid *Brezhnev* of the USSR. It led directly to the *Strategic Arms Limitation Treaty* (SALT I) of 1972.

● *Détente* enabled Nixon to isolate North Vietnam diplomatically, enabling the USA to sign a peace treaty on Vietnam in 1973.

● It led to the Helsinki Accords in 1975 on protecting human rights in eastern Europe.

● *Détente* did not end international rivalry between the two superpowers, which flared up in the *Yom Kippur War* (1973) and the civil war in Angola (1974–75). It came to an end with the Soviet invasion of *Afghanistan* in 1979.

■ TIP Questions on the course of the *Cold War* will expect a knowledge of the *détente* era and its limitations.

Diem, Ngo Dinh: dictator of South Vietnam, 1956–63.

● In a country with a Buddhist majority, Diem led a government dominated by a Catholic minority. By 1962 this government had become unpopular, largely because of corruption. It was also undermined by the communist *guerrilla* war led by the *Vietcong*.

- In an attempt to stabilise South Vietnam, Diem was overthrown by a *CIA*-sponsored army plot in 1963.
- Diem's death led to increased political instability in South Vietnam. In 1965 President *Johnson* was forced to commit ground troops, to prevent a communist take-over.

■ *TIP* The failure of Diem's regime was an important factor in explaining increased US involvement in Vietnam.

Dien Bien Phu, Battle of, 1954: a crushing defeat of the French Army by the *Vietminh* in the *Vietnam War*.

- At the *Geneva Accords* (1954) it was agreed that the French would withdraw from Indo-China and that the independent communist state of North Vietnam would be created, under the leadership of *Ho Chi Minh*.

■ *TIP* This battle is important in explaining how and why the USA became more involved in Vietnam. Following French withdrawal, the USA became the chief financial and political supporter of the non-communist state of South Vietnam.

Directory: French Revolutionary government (1795–99), formed after the fall of *Robespierre*.

- Political power in France passed to five directors and a Council of Five Hundred. The Directory period of moderate government, following the *Terror* and radicalism of 1792–94, is chiefly associated with disorganised provincial rule, French military victories in Italy and peasant revolts in the Vendée.
- The Directory was overthrown in November 1799 (*Coup of 18th Brumaire*) by *Napoleon* and his supporters.

■ *TIP* Questions often expect you to explain why the Directory lasted such a short time and what benefits it brought to France.

Disraeli, Benjamin: British Prime Minister (1868 and 1874–80), who supported development of the British empire and was a friend to the *Ottoman* (Turkish) *empire*.

- In the early stages of the *Great Eastern Crisis* of 1875–78 his main foreign policy aim was to disrupt the *League of the Three Emperors*, which he saw as a threat to Britain's interests in Europe. He threatened war against Russia in 1878 over the *Eastern Question*.
- He effectively defended British interests at the Congress of Berlin, where he prevented the collapse of the Ottoman empire and gained Cyprus as a British possession.
- In imperial affairs, he was associated with the war against Afghanistan (1878–79) and the Zulu War in South Africa (1879).

■ *TIP* Disraeli attempted to follow Lord *Palmerston*'s style of foreign policy. This was successful in Europe, but Britain faced military setbacks in the Afghan and Zulu wars.

d

Doenitz, Karl: the admiral in charge of U-boats during the Second World War, who became Commander-in-Chief of the German Navy in 1943. He was briefly *Hitler*'s successor, becoming leader of Germany in May 1945.

- In the closing years of the war Doenitz was responsible for the evacuation of millions of Germans from eastern Europe, before the arrival of the *Red Army*.
- He was tried at the Nuremberg War Trials and found guilty, serving 10 years' imprisonment.
- *TIP* He was the admiral in charge of the Battle of the Atlantic, who surrendered unconditionally to the Allies in May 1945.

domino theory: a theory underpinning US foreign policy during the *Cold War*, which postulated that, if one state fell to communism, surrounding states would quickly follow.

- The theory was first put forward by President *Eisenhower* in 1954 to explain US policy towards Indo-China. It was followed by both *Kennedy* and *Johnson*.
- It explains why the USA was committed to defending South Vietnam and Laos against communism. In 1975, when South Vietnam fell to communism, Laos and Cambodia quickly followed.
- *TIP* The theory is central to any explanation of why the USA was politically and militarily involved in Southeast Asia from 1954 to 1973.

Dreyfus, Alfred: a French Army captain at the centre of a major scandal, which rocked the Third Republic (1894–99).

- Dreyfus was charged with giving away military secrets to the Germans. As he was a Jew, this led to a wave of *anti-Semitism* in France.
- In 1899 the real culprit, Major Esterhazy, was uncovered, leading to the release of Dreyfus from prison.
- The scandal split France into Dreyfusard and anti-Dreyfusard factions. Anti-Dreyfusards contained supporters in the Army, the Catholic Church and anti-Semitic groups.
- *TIP* Questions on the stability of the Third French Republic before 1914 will involve coverage of this major scandal.

Dual Alliance, 1879–1918: a secret military alliance between Germany and Austria-Hungary.

- This was the first plank in *Bismarck*'s military/political alliance system.
- Each side agreed to support the other if war developed involving more than two opponents. The terms of the treaty would be divulged only if war was imminent. The terms of the alliance were shown to Russia in 1886, at the height of the *Bulgarian Crisis*.
- The alliance was extended in 1882 to include Italy, making it the *Triple Alliance*. Romania became an associate member in 1883.
- Britain was offered associate membership in 1889, but declined.
- *TIP* The treaty was central to Bismarck's foreign policy and bound up with the origins of the First World War. It came into effect in August 1914, when Germany and Austria-Hungary went to war with France, Russia and Britain.

Dulles, John Foster: US Secretary of State (1953–59), who developed a policy of brinkmanship under *Eisenhower*, whereby the USA threatened the use of nuclear weapons against the communist bloc as a diplomatic tactic. It was used in disputes between communist and nationalist China (1954) over Quemoy and the Matsu islands.

- Dulles pursued a strong anti-communist line. He agreed with the use of the *CIA* to overthrow foreign heads of state. The CIA was led at this time by his brother, Allen Dulles.

■ *TIP* Dulles is a central figure in the evolution of US foreign policy between *Truman* and *Kennedy*.

Duma: the lower house of the Russian national parliament, created by the *October Manifesto* of 1905.

- The first two Dumas (1906–07) demanded radical reforms from the government. However, the third Duma (1907–12) was elected on a narrower base of wealthy voters. This passed important land reforms under the guidance of the Prime Minister, *Stolypin*.

- It was suspended during the First World War, but unofficial Duma committees continued to operate. It became the basis for the *Provisional Government* after the *February Revolution of 1917*.

- The Duma was resurrected following the fall of the *USSR* in 1991.

■ *TIP* Questions requiring an explanation of the fall of Tsar *Nicholas II* will involve discussion of the Duma.

Eastern Question: a term given to a number of international problems associated with the decline of the *Ottoman* (Turkish) *empire*.

- The Ottoman empire occupied much of southeast Europe and the Middle East in the eighteenth and nineteenth centuries. Several *Great Powers*, most notably Russia and Austria, were keen to acquire Ottoman territory.
- For much of the nineteenth century, Britain attempted to prevent, or slow down, the decline of Ottoman rule.
- The Eastern Question also involved the rise of Balkan nationalism. Racial groups such as Greeks, Serbs and Bulgars fought for the creation of their own national states.
- The *Greek Revolt* (1821–32), the *Mehemet Ali* crises (1831–33 and 1839–41), the *Crimean War* (1853–56), the *Great Eastern Crisis* (1875–78), the *Bulgarian Crisis* (1885–87), the *Bosnian Crisis* (1908–09) and the *Balkan Wars* (1912–13) were all part of the foreign policy problem known as the Eastern Question.
- The *July Crisis* of 1914, which led to the First World War, was also an issue associated with this term.
- **TIP** The Eastern Question was a central issue in international relations and foreign policy. It was the most important and recurring issue involving Austria, Russia and Britain between 1815 and 1918.

Ebert, Friedrich: German President (1919–25) and member of the Social Democrat Party, who was closely associated with the signing of the Treaty of Versailles.

- He survived the political and economic crises which affected Germany between 1919 and 1923. He used the *Freikorps* to suppress a *Spartacist* (communist) uprising in 1919. This led to a permanent split between the socialists and communists in Germany.
- **TIP** Ebert represented a link between *William II* and *Weimar* Germany. His moderate use of Article 48 of the Constitution stood in marked contrast to that of his successor, *Hindenburg*.

Ebert–Groener Pact, 1918: an agreement between the head of the government, *Ebert*, and the head of the German Army, Groener.

- Ebert agreed to leave the German officer corps intact, in return for the Army's acceptance of the *Weimar Republic*.

e

- The agreement maintained the German militaristic tradition, but ensured that the Army did not become involved in politics.
- **TIP** The Pact was important in preserving the German Army after the defeat of the First World War, while allowing the Weimar Republic to establish itself without military interference.

EEC: see *European Economic Community*.

EFTA: see *European Free Trade Area*.

Eichmann, Adolf: a leading SS officer who supervised the deportation of Hungarian Jews to the Auschwitz *death camp* during 1944.

- He joined the *SD* (1934), becoming head of the office for Jewish emigration, and was responsible for the expulsion of Jews from Austria and Bohemia (1938).
- He attended the *Wannsee Conference* (1942), which launched the systematic extermination of Jews and gypsies.
- After the war he escaped from Germany, but was captured by Israeli secret agents in Argentina (1960). He was tried and executed in Israel for crimes against humanity.
- **TIP** Eichmann was a leading figure in the administration of the *Final Solution*.

Einsatzgruppen: special German police units engaged in the mass murder of Jews and communists during the invasion of the *USSR* (1941).

- They entered Russia behind the advancing German Army, with express orders to seek out Jews and communists and shoot them.
- They were responsible for the Babi Yar massacre of 33,700 Ukrainian Jews outside Kiev in 1941.
- In his book **Hitler's Willing Executioners**, historian Daniel Goldhagen stated that many **Einsatzkommando** were ordinary Germans, not necessarily committed Nazis.
- **TIP** This was a group that was engaged in the mass murder of Jews, even before the *Wannsee Conference* (1942) established the programme of *death camps*.

Eisenhower, Dwight: US President (1953–61), who ended the *Korean War* and followed a policy of *containment* of communism in Europe and Asia.

- 'Ike' (as he was popularly known) was a moderate Republican, who supported a *New Look foreign policy* from 1953 onwards. He offered financial aid to South Vietnam (1954), but took no steps to intervene in the *Hungarian Uprising* (1956).
- He used the *CIA* to overthrow governments in Iran and Guatemala.
- He placed great emphasis on nuclear weapons as the main form of defence.
- **TIP** Eisenhower's period in office saw the *Cold War* firmly established between the USA and *USSR*.

El Alamein, Battle of, 1942: a crucial battle between Allied forces, under Montgomery, and Axis forces, under Rommel, which became a turning-point in the war in North Africa.

- It led to the British conquest of Libya and Tunisia, and was the first major British land victory over the Germans. It also led to the invasion of Italy in 1943.

TIP Along with the Battle of *Stalingrad*, this battle was the turning-point in the fortunes of the Allies during the Second World War in Europe.

Emancipation of Serfs, 1861: an imperial decree made by Tsar *Alexander II* freeing all Russian serfs.

- Serfs, who comprised 80% of the population, were no longer to be the personal property of their owners.
- In compensation, the owners received redemption payments, which the serfs had to pay over 25 years.
- Serfs did not become completely free. They were placed under the control of the elders of their villages, who had the power to redistribute land.

TIP This was the most important reform of the 'Tsar Liberator'. However, it did not prevent further agricultural problems in Russia. A large increase in the rural population after 1861 resulted in periodic famine and peasant uprisings (*jacqueries*).

Emergency Banking Relief Act, 1933: enacted in an attempt to restore confidence to the US banking industry during the first *New Deal*. President *Roosevelt* closed all banks for 4 days to give the US Treasury time to produce emergency legislation.

- All banks threatened with collapse were investigated. The *Reconstruction Finance Corporation* was authorised to take over banks' debts. Solvent banks were then allowed to reopen.

TIP The impact of this measure was to save the US banking system from collapse. The act was followed up by other legislation, such as the *Glass–Steagall Act* (1933), which provided for longer-term reform.

Ems telegram, 1870: a telegram initiated by the King of Prussia, which refused the French government's demand that a member of the Prussian royal family should not become a candidate for the Spanish throne. It was the immediate cause of the *Franco–Prussian War* of 1870–71.

- *Bismarck*, the Prussian Minister-President, deliberately edited the telegram in order to cause insult to the French.
- In reply to the telegram, the French declared war in July 1870.

TIP There is some controversy over Bismarck's motives, but the French government seemed determined to go to war with Prussia in 1870.

Enabling Act, 1933: a German emergency law, passed by the *Reichstag*, which gave *Hitler* dictatorial powers for 6 months.

- The law was passed only because communist deputies were forbidden to vote. It was opposed by the *Social Democrat Party* (SPD).

TIP This was the most important development following Hitler's appointment as Chancellor in creating a Nazi dictatorship. After this act was passed, Hitler ruled without the need to summon the Reichstag to pass laws.

Entente Cordiale, 1904: an agreement between France and Britain, which ended colonial disputes in Egypt, Morocco, Thailand and the South Pacific.

- Germany feared closer relations between Britain and France and, in retaliation to the entente, created the first *Moroccan Crisis* of 1905–06 to split Britain from France. However, Britain supported French claims in Morocco.

■ *TIP* This was an important development in Britain's move away from diplomatic isolation. It brought Britain closer to France and increased British fears of Germany.

ERM: see *Exchange Rate Mechanism*.

Estates General, 1789: a national assembly, representing the monarchy, the nobility and clergy, and the 'Third Estate' (the middle class, workers and peasants), called for the first time since 1614 by *Louis XVI*, as a result of the economic crisis facing France.

● Instead of meeting the King's financial requests, the Third Estate demanded major reforms.

■ *TIP* Calling the Estates General was a major factor in setting off the French Revolution. It began 2 months later with the fall of the Bastille.

EU: see *European Union*.

euro: a new currency for the *European Union*, launched in 1999 and designated to become the official currency by 2002.

● Only Britain, Denmark and Greece did not join the euro currency system in 1999.

● The possibility of abandoning the pound sterling in favour of the euro has resulted in intense political debate in Britain.

■ *TIP* The prospect of joining the euro has become a major stumbling block to further integration of Britain into the EU.

European Commission: the organisation in Brussels which runs the *European Union*, administering the *Common Agricultural Policy*, the Regional Development Fund and other EU institutions.

● The organisation is run by a group of commissioners chosen from the member states.

● In 2000 Britain had two commissioners, former Conservative minister Chris Patten and former Labour leader Neil Kinnock.

■ *TIP* The Commission has been criticised because it is unelected and the European Parliament has limited control of its activities.

European Economic Community (EEC): the economic union created by the Treaty of *Rome* (1957).

● It originally contained six members (France, Italy, West Germany, Holland, Belgium and Luxembourg), and was expanded in 1973 to include Britain, Ireland and Denmark, and in 1981 to include Greece. The EEC was forerunner to the *European Union*.

■ *TIP* The creation of the EEC was central to the development of west European integration. Although it began as an economic organisation, demands for political integration, and ultimate union, became much stronger in the closing decade of the twentieth century.

European Free Trade Association (EFTA): set up in 1959 as a counterweight to the *EEC*, it included Britain, Austria, Denmark, Norway, Sweden, Portugal and Switzerland.

- It created an alternative free trade zone. The organisation was undermined by the decision of Britain and Denmark to join the EEC in 1973, which Sweden, Austria and Portugal also subsequently joined.

TIP Originally an important trade group for Britain, it was ultimately undermined by growth of the *European Union*.

European Union (EU): an economic and political union of European states, which began as the *European Economic Community* in 1957 with the signing of the Treaty of *Rome*.

- It originally contained six members: West Germany, France, Italy, Holland, Belgium and Luxembourg. It is now expanded to 15 states, including Britain and the Republic of Ireland.
- Plans to expand membership further and to increase economic and political union are the cause of intense debate in the European Union, in particular in Britain.

TIP The European Union is the central and most important organisation in the move towards European integration. Other organisations which have increased European integration since 1945 are the *European Free Trade Association* and the *Council of Europe*.

Exchange Rate Mechanism (ERM): an agreement within the *European Union*, which aimed to link the value of EU currencies to the value of the German mark, in an attempt to bolster financial stability.

- Britain joined in 1990, but was forced to leave in 1992 because of the inability of the pound sterling to keep its value against the German mark.
- The ERM was a prelude to the creation of a single European currency, the *euro*.

TIP The ERM was part of a process to create currency stability in a period of flexible exchange rates. The ERM crisis of 1992 undermined the Conservative government of John Major and led to the resignation of his Chancellor of the Exchequer, Norman Lamont.

Executive Office of the Presidency, 1939: an office created as a result of an expansion in the role of President and of the US government during the *New Deal*.

- It included the Office of Management and Budget, which assisted the President in the production of the Federal Budget.
- Its creation met with opposition, due to fears that *Roosevelt* was acquiring too much power. The proposal was rejected by the House of Representatives in 1938, but passed by Presidential Executive Order the following year.

TIP It became a permanent feature of presidential politics. In 1947 the National Security Council was added to the Executive Office.

Fair Labor Standards Act, 1938: fixed a minimum wage and maximum hours of work in all industries involved in US interstate commerce.

- The minimum wage was set at 25 cents per hour, with an aim to raise it to 40 cents per hour. Maximum hours were set at 44 hours per week, with an aim to reduce this to 40 hours within 3 years.
- Child labour under 16 was forbidden and 16–18 year olds were forbidden to work in hazardous employment. Unfortunately, domestic servants and farm labourers were exempt from the legislation.
- **TIP** *Roosevelt's* administration was able to use federal powers over interstate commerce (commerce between states) to pass the act, whereas it had no jurisdiction over intrastate commerce (commerce within a single state).

fascist: a member of *Mussolini's* political party, founded in Italy in 1919.

- Fascists were anti-democratic, anti-socialist and nationalist.
- They believed in action, and demanded that Italy should receive its rightful place as a major European power with a large colonial empire.
- The term later came to be used to describe right-wing, anti-democratic parties, such as the Falange in Spain and the Nazis in Germany.

Fashoda Incident, 1898: an African colonial crisis involving Britain and France in the Sudan.

- Britain claimed sovereignty over the whole of the Nile Valley, including the Sudan. In 1896 Lord Kitchener led an Anglo–Egyptian army to conquer the Sudan.
- At Fashoda Kitchener met with the forces of Captain Marchand of France, who also claimed part of the Sudan for France.
- This led to an international crisis, in which the British mobilised their fleet in preparation for war. The French government, caught in the middle of the *Dreyfus* scandal, backed down, allowing Britain to occupy the whole of the Sudan.
- **TIP** A colonial clash in the partition of Africa, it was the last major confrontation between Britain and France before the First World War.

February Revolution of 1848 in France: brought about by economic recession, a desire for political reform and the unpopularity of *Guizot's* ministry, and led to the fall of King *Louis Philippe*.

- It centred on Paris, where a mob took control of the city. The National Guard sided with the revolutionaries.
- A Second French Republic was declared, which adopted socialist policies such as the establishment of the *National Workshops.*
- *TIP* Questions often probe the unplanned, accidental nature of the fall of Louis Philippe's regime.

February Revolution of 1917 in Russia: brought on by the pressures of fighting a major European war and led to the fall of the tsarist regime and the creation of a Russian republic.

- By 1917 Russia was losing the war on the Eastern Front.
- Unrest began with demonstrations about food shortages and prices. These escalated into revolution, with the support of dissident army units and workers in *Petrograd*, capital of the Russian empire.
- An unofficial committee of the *Duma* asked Tsar *Nicholas II* to abdicate. He abdicated for himself and his young son, Alexis.
- *TIP* This revolution was spontaneous and the *Bolsheviks* played virtually no part in it.

Federal Emergency Relief Act, 1933: an attempt to provide relief for the unemployed in the USA during the Depression.

- The act created the Federal Emergency Relief Administration (FERA), which was allocated $500 million to be divided among the states to help the unemployed.
- FERA was placed under the leadership of Harry Hopkins, who used the threat of cutting off all federal aid to states who would not comply with its conditions, such as Kentucky and Ohio.
- *TIP* FERA had a limited effect on overcoming the impact of the Depression. It faced considerable opposition from some states. In 1935 FERA relief amounted to $25 a month — when the lowest working wage was about $100.

Federal Housing Act, 1934: an attempt to increase housing construction in the USA by offering federal insurance on low-interest and long-term mortgages taken out to buy new homes.

- It created the Federal Housing Administration (FHA), but did little to assist inner-city areas, encouraging only movement to the suburbs.
- It mainly benefited the white, middle class. Only 25% of urban families could afford the kind of mortgage offered under the act.
- *TIP* This measure, which was part of the first *New Deal*, had little impact on the poorer sections of society, helping only middle-class America.

feminism: a political and social movement, which began in the USA, demanding equality for women.

- Feminism as a movement rose to prominence during the 1960s, with the National Organisation for Women (NOW), which helped to pressure the US *Congress* into passing Schedule VII of the *Civil Rights Act* (1964) guaranteeing equality for women.

- It also led to demands for the Equal Rights Amendment (ERA), which almost became part of the US Constitution in the early 1970s.
- The term is now used to describe women's organisations across the world which seek political, civil and social equality between the sexes.
- **TIP** The changing social and economic status of women became a major issue in the history of the USA after 1945.

Final Solution: the German plan to exterminate European Jews and gypsies during the Second World War.

- Controversy still surrounds the plan. Did *Hitler* intend to carry out the Final Solution all along, or was it a result of the war?
- It began officially with the *Wannsee Conference* (1942) in Berlin. The policy was carried out by the *SS* under Heinrich *Himmler*.
- By 1945 6 million Jews and 500,000 gypsies had been exterminated.
- **TIP** The Final Solution (also known as the Holocaust or Shoah) was a central and controversial part of Nazi policy.

First Republic, France, 1792–1804: created following the flight of *Louis XVI* to *Varennes* and marked the final overthrow of the *ancien régime*.

- It introduced the new Revolutionary calendar, with 1792 as Year 1. It was also associated with the Revolutionary *Terror*.
- The Republic entered its most radical phase in 1793–94, with the rule of *Robespierre*.
- The *Thermidorian Reaction* (1794–95) led to the creation of the more moderate *Directory*.
- The last phase of the Republic was associated with the rise of *Napoleon*, who abolished it in 1804, proclaiming instead the First French Empire.
- **TIP** The First Republic was the period of French history most closely associated with extreme political views. In 1830, 1848 and 1871, French revolutionaries looked back to this period as the example to follow if their revolutions were to succeed.

Fiume: a seaport on the Adriatic, the location for *D'Annunzio*'s occupation and government (1919–21). It became a Free City under the League of Nations in 1924 (later the port of Rijeka in Croatia).

Five Year Plans: industrial plans for the central direction of the Soviet economy, first introduced by *Stalin* in 1928.

- The communist leaders believed that, with systematic economic planning, they could turn the *USSR* into a modern industrial state.
- Industrial targets were set for all industries by *Gosplan*, the central planning organisation.
- The first Five Year Plan ran from 1928 to 1933, the second from 1933 to 1937. A Third Plan, begun in 1937, was cut short by the outbreak of the Second World War. A Fourth Plan was begun after the war.
- The Plans led to rapid industrialisation and brought about a strong Soviet economy, but this was created in part by slave labour from the *Gulag* concentration camps.

▌ *TIP* The Five Year Plans are central to any study of Stalin's rule in the USSR from 1928 onwards.

Florida land boom: a speculative land boom which mushroomed in the 1920s.

- It began as a result of the development of the motor car, which allowed easy access to the state of Florida.
- Between 1920 and 1925 the population of Florida increased from about 950,000 to 1.2 million. People began to speculate in unseen land development, with the expectation of making large profits.
- The boom collapsed in 1926 after hurricanes devastated parts of Florida and speculators discovered that many land plots were simply swampland.

▌ *TIP* Along with the stock market boom, this is a fine example of the speculation which destabilised the US economy in the 1920s.

Ford, Gerald: US President (1974–77), who succeeded *Nixon* following his resignation over the *Watergate Scandal* and pardoned him, thus keeping the former President from jail.

- During his presidency, South Vietnam, Laos and Cambodia fell to communism. In Africa, Portugal gave independence to its colonies, which established socialist and communist regimes.

Fordney–McCumber Tariff, 1922: a measure which led to a large increase in US import duties (tariffs).

- Duties were raised on farm products, chemicals, textiles and other industrial goods.
- The Federal Trade Commission was instructed to examine production costs and make recommendations to the President, so that he might make revisions to the tariff.

▌ *TIP* This was a major intervention in the economy by the US government, in an era noted for laissez-faire economics (a policy involving minimal government intervention in the economy). Tariffs were increased again with the *Hawley–Smoot Tariff* of 1930.

Fourteen Points: US aims for the postwar world put forward by President *Wilson* in January 1918.

- Woodrow Wilson's statement made four general points, calling for open diplomacy, freedom of the seas, international free trade and universal disarmament.
- There were a number of specific points, which included the return of Alsace-Lorraine to France, Belgian independence and the restoration of Balkan states such as Serbia.
- The final point suggested the creation of a 'league of nations' after the war, to maintain peace.

▌ *TIP* When agreeing to an armistice in November 1918, Germany believed that the peace treaty would be based on the Fourteen Points. However, the *Paris Peace* Settlement proved far harsher for the defeated Central Powers.

Four Year Plan, 1936: a German economic plan to achieve *autarky* (economic self-sufficiency) in preparation for war.

f

- *Goering* was put in control of the Plan, which involved massive rearmament and the creation of synthetic products, such as rubber and oil from coal.
- **TIP** The Four Year Plan met with limited success, with Germany facing another economic crisis in 1938. This was offset by the outbreak of war with Poland in September 1939.

Franco, Francisco: Spanish soldier and statesman who led the nationalist forces to victory in the Spanish Civil War (1936–39), and who subsequently ruled Spain until 1975.

- He created a right-wing, authoritarian regime, destroying Spanish socialism and communism.
- Known as El Caudillo (The Leader), he created a one-party state where the Falange Party was given exclusive power.
- In the 1960s he developed diplomatic links with the USA, allowing US bases on Spanish soil.
- His death in 1975 led to the restoration of the Spanish monarchy under King Juan Carlos. It also led to the creation of Spanish democracy and the modernisation of Spanish society.
- **TIP** Franco is a classic example of a right-wing military leader, who took control of his country's government in interwar Europe. Others include Admiral Horthy in Hungary and Marshal Pilsudski in Poland.

Franco–Prussian War, 1870–71: a defeat for France, which led to the fall of the Second Empire of *Napoleon III* and the unification of Germany under Prussia.

- The French declared war following receipt of the *Ems telegram* from *Bismarck*.
- A Prussian victory was secured through superior military tactics and organisation. The decisive battle took place at Sedan, in September 1870, resulting in the capture of the French Emperor and the siege of Paris. The war ended with the Treaty of *Frankfurt*, France losing Alsace-Lorraine to Germany.
- **TIP** The war brought about a fundamental change in the European balance of power, with Germany becoming the dominant *Great Power*. In France, the Third Republic was declared, which was followed by a short civil war and the Paris *Commune*.

Frank, Anne: a victim of Nazi persecution who, as a teenage girl, kept a diary of her life in hiding. The diary was published after the war and became one of the most famous testimonies of life during the Holocaust in Holland.

- The Franks were a German Jewish family, who moved to Amsterdam following the Nazi rise to power. After the German occupation of Holland in May 1940, the family lived in hiding.
- They were finally discovered and arrested by the *Gestapo*. They all died in a concentration camp. Anne was just 16 years old.
- **TIP** The diary constitutes important evidence of life in the shadow of the *Final Solution*.

Frankfurt, Treaty of, 1871: ended the *Franco–Prussian War* of 1870–71.

- The main term was the transfer of Alsace-Lorraine from France to Germany. This caused conflict between the two states until the end of the First World War.
- France was also forced to accept an army of occupation until it paid a large war indemnity. This was completed in 1875 and led to the *War in Sight Crisis*, when *Bismarck* threatened France with a preventive war.
- ▮ *TIP* The terms of this treaty were the main cause of Franco–German enmity after 1871. French resentment resulted in Bismarck's attempt to isolate France internationally between 1871 and 1890.

Frankfurt Parliament, 1848–49: a liberal parliament established as a result of the 1848 revolutions in Germany.

- Liberals from all the German states met to discuss how to create a united Germany.
- Division occurred between those who wanted to include Austria (the *Grossdeutschland* solution) and those who wanted to exclude Austria, with Prussia as the dominant state (the *Kleindeutschland* solution).
- The parliament eventually chose the latter. It failed to unite Germany though, because it lacked military power and was opposed by the German monarchs.
- ▮ *TIP* The meeting of the Frankfurt Parliament was a major aspect of the 1848 revolutions in Germany. The failure of the liberals left *Bismarck* and Prussia to unite Germany by military means in the 1860s.

freedom rides: an attempt to desegregate interstate bus services in the Old South.

- Organised by the Congress for Racial Equality in 1961, Black and White students from elsewhere in the USA deliberately broke segregation rules in bus station waiting rooms to highlight inequality.
- These actions prompted considerable violence by Southern Whites. Intervention by the US Attorney-General, Robert F. Kennedy, finally led to a solution.
- ▮ *TIP* The 'freedom rides' are a good example of how African Americans and their liberal White sympathisers, by their own actions, attempted to desegregate the recalcitrant states of the Old South.

Freikorps: groups of nationalist ex-servicemen in the *Weimar Republic*, who were used savagely to suppress the *Spartacist* (communist) uprising in Berlin in January 1919.

- In March 1920 they attempted to overthrow the democratic government by supporting the *Kapp Putsch*. They also fought Polish nationalists in Upper Silesia during the *League of Nations plebiscite* (1921).
- Many *Freikorps* members subsequently joined the Nazi Party.
- ▮ *TIP* Note that the existence of the *Freikorps* showed up the weakness of the early Weimar Republic.

Fundamental Law of 1906: an imperial decree in Russia, following publication of the *October Manifesto* of 1905, which created the first Russian constitution and national parliament, the *Duma*.

- The constitution fell far short of the October Manifesto. Article 87 enabled the tsar to rule by decree when the Duma was not in session. The constitution also gave the tsar the power to appoint and dismiss the government, control the Army and conduct foreign policy.

■ *TIP* The Fundamental Law showed that the tsar still retained most political power in Russia. Demands for political reform continued.

gangsterism: the rise of organised crime in the USA in the 1920s, associated primarily with *Prohibition*.
- Huge profits could be made from bootlegging (making and selling illegal alcohol).
- Centred on Chicago, gangsters ran 'speakeasy' bars and smuggled alcoholic drinks from Canada. To maintain control of their illegal businesses, the gangsters bribed and intimidated police, judges and politicians.
- The most notorious gangster was Al Capone. In 1929 his gang murdered a group of rivals in the infamous St Valentine's Day Massacre.
- *TIP* Gangsterism undermined support for Prohibition and was a cause of its eventual repeal in 1933.

Garibaldi, Giuseppe: an Italian nationalist leader, who conquered Sicily and Naples in 1860 in the cause of Italian unity.
- He had fought in 1849 to defend the Roman Republic and in 1859 for Piedmont-Sardinia against Austria.
- He handed his conquests of Sicily and Naples to King Victor Emanuel II of Piedmont-Sardinia, thereby creating a united Italy.
- After the creation of the Kingdom of Italy in 1861, Garibaldi twice tried to invade Rome, in 1864 and 1867. Both attempts were unsuccessful.
- *TIP* Garibaldi stands in marked contrast to Piedmontese Prime Minister *Cavour*. Garibaldi was in favour of a united, democratic Italy; Cavour wanted to make Piedmont-Sardinia the dominant north Italian state.

Gastein Agreement, 1865: an agreement between Austria and Prussia over Schleswig-Holstein, which resulted in conflict between them and led to the *Seven Weeks War* of 1866.
- Schleswig was placed under Prussian administration and Holstein under Austria.
- *TIP* The agreement was an important part of *Bismarck*'s diplomacy. He used the Schleswig-Holstein issue to force Austria to accept Prussia as an equal in Germany, or go to war.

Geneva Accords, 1954: an international agreement on Indo-China, involving the *USSR*, the USA, Britain and France, which ended the French colonial presence.

g

- It was agreed to divide Indo-China into four states. Laos and Cambodia became independent, neutral kingdoms.
- North Vietnam became a communist state, while South Vietnam remained pro-West. Provision was made for nationwide elections in all Vietnam in 1956, as a prelude to unity. The elections were cancelled at the insistence of the USA, because they feared a communist victory.
- **TIP** The Geneva Accords were an important stage in the growing involvement of the USA in Southeast Asia. After 1954 the USA openly supported South Vietnam.

Geneva Protocol, 1924: an international agreement designed to strengthen the powers of the *League of Nations*.

- All signatories to the Protocol were required to accept the peaceful arbitration of international disputes.
- It was supported by the British Labour Prime Minister Ramsay MacDonald.
- **TIP** The Protocol should be seen, along with the *Kellogg–Briand Pact* of 1928, as an attempt to encourage peaceful solutions to international disputes.

German Confederation (*Bund*), 1815–66: an organisation of 39 German states, including the two *Great Powers* of Austria and Prussia, which was created by the Treaty of *Vienna* and replaced the Holy Roman Empire and the Confederation of the Rhine.

- An assembly (Diet) of states met in Frankfurt under the direction of Austria, but it had little power.
- The Confederation was used by the Austrian Chancellor, *Metternich*, to suppress German liberalism between 1815 and 1848.
- It collapsed in the *Seven Weeks War* between Austria and Prussia. It was partially replaced by the Prussian-dominated *North German Confederation* of 1867.
- **TIP** The **Bund** failed to provide political stability in central Europe, chiefly because of rivalry between Austria and Prussia and the demand for liberalism.

German Constitution of 1871: created by *Bismarck* for the new German empire, to ensure Prussian dominance.

- The King of Prussia was German Emperor and commander of the armed forces. He appointed and dismissed the imperial government.
- The upper house of the national parliament, the **Bundesrat,** was dominated by Prussian delegates. Prussia also comprised some two-thirds of the new empire.
- However, the lower house (the *Reichstag*) was elected by universal male suffrage (vote). Conflict between the democratically elected Reichstag and conservative governments became a feature of the second German empire (1871–1918).
- **TIP** Any study of German domestic politics between 1871 and 1918 should begin with an analysis of how the German political system worked.

Gestapo: the secret state police of Nazi Germany.

- In 1934 the Gestapo was placed under the control of Heinrich *Himmler*, the head of the *SS*.

g

- It was responsible for arresting political opponents of the Nazi regime, not just in Germany, but also in German-occupied Europe during the Second World War.

■ *TIP* Do not confuse the Gestapo with the SS, which operated concentration and *death camps*.

Giap, Vo Nguyen: a Vietnamese communist military commander, who was a leading exponent of *guerrilla warfare* against the French (1946–54) and the Americans (1965–73).

- He led the *Vietminh* forces which defeated the French at the Battle of *Dien Bien Phu*, in 1954. He was Commander of the North Vietnamese Army (NVA) during the war against the USA in South Vietnam and surrounded the US Marine Corps base at Khe Sanh in 1968. Following the military failure of the *Tet Offensive* in 1968, the NVA took on a greater burden of the war from the *Vietcong*.

■ *TIP* Giap was a leading architect of the communist victory in Vietnam.

Girondins: middle-class republicans in the French Legislative Assembly (1792) and the Convention (1793).

- They supported the Revolutionary War against Austria and Prussia, but opposed the methods used by the *Jacobins*.
- The group was destroyed through arrests and the execution of its leaders, such as Brissot and Petion, in 1794. It took its name from the Gironde area of southwest France, from where many of its supporters originally came.

■ *TIP* Understanding the political position of the various republican groups in France (1792–94) is important in any explanation of how the Revolution developed.

Gladstone, William: British statesman and Prime Minister (1868–74, 1880–85, 1886 and 1892–94), who was opposed to excessive military expenditure and in favour of the *Concert of Europe* and international arbitration.

- During his first ministry Gladstone resolved international conflicts peacefully, particularly over the Russian decision to revoke the Black Sea clauses of the Treaty of *Paris* and the Alabama Case. In his second ministry he resolved the Montenegro and Greek border disputes through the Concert of Europe.
- However, during 1880–85 his government was most closely associated with the rapid expansion of British territory in Africa.
- He resigned as Prime Minister in 1894, because he opposed a rise in expenditure on the Royal Navy.

■ *TIP* Gladstone attempted to pursue a peaceful foreign policy, but his efforts to use the Concert of Europe after 1880 were thwarted by *Bismarck*'s alliance system.

glasnost: a Russian term meaning 'openness', which was especially associated with the rule of Mikhail *Gorbachev* (1985–91).

- *Glasnost* was introduced as part of a programme to improve the performance of the Soviet economy. It was linked to the policy of *perestroika* (restructuring). The press became freer and industries became self-managing.

- The policy had little impact on the Soviet economy, but it did encourage the growth of nationalism in the Baltic Republics and the Caucasus region.
- ▦ *TIP* *Glasnost* signalled important changes in policy in the final years of the *USSR* and was central to Gorbachev's attempt to move away from propaganda and be more honest with his own people.

Glass–Steagall Banking Act, 1933: an attempt to reform the US banking system following the Depression by prohibiting high-street banks from involvement with investment banking. This had fuelled speculation in stocks and shares before the *Wall Street Crash*.

- Bank officials were forbidden to take out personal loans from their own banks. Buying and selling of government shares and bonds was transferred to the Federal Reserve Board.
- To administer these changes the Federal Deposit Insurance Corporation (FDIC) was created.
- ▦ *TIP* The act was an important part of the first *New Deal*.

Gleichschaltung: a term meaning 'forcible coordination', used to describe the creation of the Nazi dictatorship in Germany between January 1933 and August 1934.

- The abolition of ***Lände*** (German state governments), the creation of the German Labour Front (to replace independent trade unions), and the creation of one-party rule were all part of this process.
- ▦ *TIP* The Nazis brought about a political revolution in Germany. Did they also, through *Gleichschaltung*, bring about a revolution in German society?

Goebbels, Josef: Nazi Minister for Propaganda and National Enlightenment, appointed in 1933.

- He controlled German radio and cinema and was an outstanding propagandist.
- In 1943 he encouraged the German war effort with his 'total war' speech in Berlin. Unlike *Hitler*, he regularly visited bombed German cities during the war.
- He committed suicide in Hitler's bunker in April 1945.
- ▦ *TIP* Goebbels's skill in propaganda was an important element in the creation of the Führer myth about Hitler.

Goering, Hermann: Nazi head of the German air force (***Luftwaffe***), ***Reichsmarshal***, and head of the Four Year Plan.

- Goering was a flamboyant and arrogant figure. He believed the ***Luftwaffe*** could defeat the RAF in the Battle of *Britain* (1940) and also that they would be able to supply the besieged Sixth Army in *Stalingrad* (1942–43); he was wrong about both.
- He lost influence with *Hitler* after 1943, with the rise of *Himmler* and *Bormann*.
- He put up an effective defence of his actions at the Nuremberg War Trials, but committed suicide after being sentenced to death.
- ▦ *TIP* Goering's quest for individual power in the Nazi state is an example of how disorganised and faction-ridden Nazi rule was under Hitler.

Gold Standard: the system whereby trade surpluses or deficits gave rise to an increase or decrease in a country's gold reserves, which was the basis of international trade from the nineteenth century to the early 1930s.

● The use of gold to back a country's currency gave confidence to the system. However, the Gold Standard was damaged by the economic effects of the First World War.

● Attempts by countries to return to the Gold Standard after the war could not be sustained. Britain returned in 1925, only to leave again in 1931. Since 1945 the US dollar has replaced gold as the world's major trading currency.

■ *TIP* The term is important in explaining the operation of international trade in the nineteenth century.

Gorbachev, Mikhail: ruler of the *USSR* (1985–91), who attempted to save the Russian economy through the twin policies of *perestroika* (restructuring) and *glasnost* (openness).

● He withdrew Soviet forces from Afghanistan and tried to reduce the number of nuclear weapons in START (the *Strategic Arms Reduction Talks*) with US presidents *Reagan* and *Bush*.

● He faced considerable opposition in the Communist Party, from conservatives led by Ligachev. His most important decision was a refusal to use the *Red Army* against democratic movements in eastern Europe in 1989. This led to the fall of communism.

● Gorbachev survived a coup to overthrow him only because of the support of *Yeltsin*. He resigned when the USSR disintegrated in 1991.

■ *TIP* Answers to questions on the end of the *Cold War* or the fall of communism must take account of Gorbachev's policies.

Gorlice–Tarnow Offensive, 1915: an attack by German and Austro-Hungarian forces, which resulted in a defeat for Russia on the Eastern Front and led to the Tsar taking personal control of the Russian Army in the field.

■ *TIP* This defeat helped to force the abdication of the Tsar in February 1917.

Gosplan: the Soviet organisation for central economic planning, established in 1921, which set and monitored economic targets during the *Five Year Plans* under *Stalin*.

● It continued to operate under Stalin's successors. However, from 1985 onwards, *Gorbachev* greatly reduced its power by allowing the self-management of factories.

■ *TIP* Gosplan effectively controlled the Soviet centrally planned economy.

Great Eastern Crisis, 1875–78: a major international crisis in the *Balkans*, which almost caused a European war.

● It began with the revolt of Christian peasants in Bosnia and Hercegovina against Turkish rule and escalated into war between Turkey and the Christian Balkan states of Serbia and Montenegro.

● Attempts by the *Great Powers* (1875–76) to end the conflict failed.

● In 1877 the imminent defeat of Serbia and Montenegro led to Russian military intervention (the Russo–Turkish War of 1877–78). The Treaty of *San Stefano,* which ended the Russo–Turkish War, led in its turn to a major confrontation between Britain and Austria-Hungary with Russia.

● The Congress of Berlin (1878) settled the crisis.

■ *TIP* This was a major conflict in the *Eastern Question*. It ended with a triumph for *Bismarck* at Berlin, acting as 'honest broker' between the Great Powers. It was also regarded as a triumph for the British Prime Minister, *Disraeli.*

Great Leap Forward: the Chinese communist attempt of 1958–60 to industrialise the country very rapidly.

● It followed a split between the *USSR* and the China of *Mao Zedong*. Attempts to produce iron and steel in village furnaces, and changes to agricultural production, proved disastrous.

● The policy caused a famine in 1960, which led to millions of deaths.

■ *TIP* The failure of the Great Leap Forward undermined Mao's authority, which he attempted to regain through the *Cultural Revolution.*

Great Power: a term in international relations used to describe the most influential countries during the eighteenth and nineteenth centuries. Great Power status was closely associated with military might.

● There were five European Great Powers: Britain, France, Austria, Russia and Prussia/Germany.

● During the nineteenth century the European *balance of power* was maintained by the Great Powers acting together in concert.

● Following the First World War the term fell into disuse. From 1945 to 1991 the world was dominated by two 'superpowers', the USA and the *USSR.*

■ *TIP* The concept is central to an understanding of nineteenth-century international relations.

Greek Revolt, 1821–32: a major event in the *Eastern Question*, following which a Greek kingdom was established by the *Great Powers* at the Treaty of London (1832).

● The Greek War of Independence led to the involvement of France, Russia and Britain. The Greeks gained independence following a Russian victory in the Russo–Turkish War of 1828–29.

■ *TIP* The creation of an independent Greek state is an example of the *Concert of Europe* in operation.

Grossdeutschland: a 'big Germany' solution to the problem of German unification, which would have involved incorporating the Austrian empire — and a large number of non-Germans, such as Hungarians.

● It was rejected by the liberal *Frankfurt Parliament* of 1848–49, in favour of a united Germany under Prussia.

Guderian, Heinz: a prominent general in the Second World War, who led German *Panzer* forces in the *blitzkrieg* on Poland in 1939, and against the West in 1940.

● He was dismissed from his post during Operation *Barbarossa*, following a dispute with *Hitler.*

- However, he was made Inspector General of Armoured Forces in 1943 and Chief of the Army General Staff following the *July Plot* of 1944. He was responsible for purging hundreds of officers from the forces following the plot.
- He died shortly after being captured by the Allies in May 1945.
- ▧ *TIP* Guderian was a leading exponent of the successful blitzkrieg tactic.

guerrilla warfare: tactics of hit-and-run raids, ambushes and assassinations, usually employed by forces which are militarily inferior to their opponents.

- The aim is generally to wear down the opposition's will and ability to continue fighting a war, by inflicting unacceptably high levels of casualties or expenditure.
- The tactics have been used successfully by liberation movements, especially the *Vietminh* and *Vietcong* forces in the *Vietnam War*, by Che Guevara in the Cuban Revolutionary War, in wars in Africa and Latin America, and in Northern Ireland by the Provisional IRA.
- ▧ *TIP* Coming into its own since the Second World War, guerrilla warfare was employed to maximum effect in Vietnam, forcing the world's greatest military power to withdraw.

Guizot, François: a French statesman during the reign of *Louis Philippe*, whose refusal to support reform led finally to the downfall of the monarchy.

- His main influence on government was felt between 1840 and 1848, although he became Prime Minister only in 1847.
- He refused to accept ministerial responsibility towards the Chamber of Deputies. As meetings had been declared illegal, 'reform banquets' were held, leading a reform movement. This coincided with a major economic recession.
- In February 1848 opposition to Guizot led not only to his political downfall, but to the downfall of the monarchy.
- ▧ *TIP* Guizot was a central figure in the fall of the 'July Monarchy'. Louis Philippe became so closely identified with Guizot that, when his Prime Minister fell, so did the King.

Gulag: the Soviet concentration camp system, set up by the *OGPU* in 1930, in which more than 2 million people died.

- Numbers held in the *Gulag* vary greatly, according to Western estimates. It has been suggested that between 2 and 20 million were incarcerated at any one time.
- Life in the *Gulag* was graphically illustrated in Alexander Solzhenitsyn's short story ***One Day in the Life of Ivan Denisovich***. Solzhenitsyn later wrote a three-volume history of the *Gulag*.
- ▧ *TIP* The indiscriminate nature of *Stalin's Purges* meant that a complete cross-section of Soviet society ended up in the camps.

Gulf War, 1991: a major international intervention against Iraq, led by the USA and caused by the Iraqi invasion of Kuwait.

- The alliance against Iraq included Arab states such as Saudi Arabia, Syria and the Gulf States. The Allied forces were immediately successful, due to superior air power and military technology. The war ended within 6 weeks.

- However, the fall of Saddam Hussein, the Iraqi leader, did not follow, as had been hoped. Conflict remained between Iraq and the Western powers, in particular the USA and Britain.

■ *TIP* The Gulf War was the first major conflict following the end of the *Cold War*. It demonstrated US military and political power in the Middle East.

Hammarskjöld, Dag: Swedish Secretary General of the *United Nations* (UN) from 1953 to 1961, who established the position of Secretary General as an independent and authoritative voice in international relations.
- Seen originally as a compromise candidate between East and West, he oversaw the first UN peacekeeping force following the *Suez Crisis* (1956).
- In 1960 he established a UN peacekeeping force in the former Belgian Congo (Democratic Republic of Congo) to help bring an end to post-colonial civil war. He was killed in the Congo in an air crash.

Harding, Warren: US President 1921–23, whose reformist administration was affected by political scandal.
- His presidency was associated with corruption, such as the Teapot Dome scandal, which involved government-owned oil reserves.
- However, Harding made important changes to the federal government, creating the Office of Management and Budget (1921).
- He signed the Washington Naval Treaty (1922), which limited naval armaments in the Pacific.

Hawley–Smoot Tariff, 1930: an increase in import duties to the USA, introduced by Herbert *Hoover*'s administration.
- Its aim was to protect US industry from foreign competition.
- It had the effect of reducing international trade and making the world-wide economic depression worse.
- *TIP* This was a Republican intervention in economic matters, which ran counter to laissez-faire (free-market) economics.

Hebertists: the most extreme group of French Republicans during the *Terror* of 1792–94.
- They took their name from Jacques Hébert, whose newspaper, *La Père Duchesne*, influenced radical opinion.
- They opposed Christianity and sought its replacement with festivals in honour of Reason.
- They were opposed to *Robespierre*'s leadership. The discovery of a plot by the Hebertists against the government led to the arrest and execution of Hébert and his chief supporters.

h

■ *TIP* Remember, the 1792–94 period of the French Revolution contains a wide variety of political groups. Make sure that you use the terms correctly.

Hess, Rudolf: deputy leader of Nazi Germany who, in 1941, flew to Britain in a bizarre attempt to persuade *Churchill* to end the war.

● He was a First World War comrade of *Hitler* and an early member of the Nazi Party. He acted as Hitler's secretary in prison, when Hitler dictated *Mein Kampf*.

● In 1938 he became one of only six members of the Ministerial Council for the Defence of the Reich.

● After landing in Scotland on his self-appointed mission he was captured and spent the rest of his life in prison. After the war he was held mostly in Spandau prison, Berlin, and achieved notoriety as the last important Nazi left alive. He died in 1987.

■ *TIP* At the time of his flight, Hess was losing influence in the Nazi Party to *Himmler, Goering* and *Goebbels*.

Heydrich, Reinhard: *Himmler's* deputy in the *SS*, who became the chief organiser of the *Final Solution*.

● He joined the Nazi Party and the SS in 1931, becoming head of the *SD* (Security Service). He was promoted following the *Night of the Long Knives* (1934) and was responsible for the *Kristallnacht* attacks on German Jews (1938).

● Appointed head of the Reich Central Office for Jewish Emigration in 1939, he organised the *Wannsee Conference* (1942), which set up the *death camp* system. He was assassinated by Czech nationalists in 1942.

■ *TIP* Heydrich, rather than Himmler, set up the apparatus for the mass extermination of Jews and gypsies.

Himmler, Heinrich: a leading Nazi, who became head of the *SS* and overseer of the *Final Solution*.

● Following the *Night of the Long Knives* (1934), the SS became the main Nazi paramilitary force and, later, administrators of the concentration camp system.

● With the outbreak of the Second World War, Himmler became Minister of the Interior and, from 1944, Commander of Home Forces, which included the **Volksturm** (Home Guard). He also became head of the **Waffen SS**, the élite force of the German Army.

● He was brought to book at the Nuremberg War Trials, but committed suicide.

■ *TIP* Himmler created his own large organisation in Germany and Nazi-occupied Europe. His activities support the view that Nazi Germany was run by a competing set of powerful leaders, not just *Hitler*.

Hindenburg, Paul von: German President 1925–34, who used Article 48 of the *Weimar* Constitution to appoint Chancellors *Brüning*, von Papen, von Schleicher and *Hitler* between 1930 and 1933.

● Made a Field Marshal in the First World War, von Hindenburg was a conservative President.

● He was re-elected in 1932, beating Hitler. He disliked Hitler, but was persuaded to appoint him Chancellor in 1933.

- He failed to criticise Hitler's government when it introduced the *Enabling Act* (1933) and suppressed the Communist Party.
- When Hindenburg died in 1934, as well as becoming Chancellor, Hitler became Head of State, calling himself 'Führer of the German people'.

▓ *TIP* Hindenburg's presidency was an important factor in allowing Hitler to take power.

Hitler, Adolf: Nazi leader and German Chancellor, 1933–45.

- Austrian by birth, Hitler served in the German Army 1914–18. He joined the Nazi party in 1919, becoming leader in 1921.
- His failed attempt to seize power in the *Beer Hall Putsch* of 1923 led to 10 months' imprisonment.
- Largely through his ability as a demagogue and his mastery of propaganda, he rose to the position of Chancellor following the Depression of 1929–33 and created a dictatorship in Germany between January 1933 and August 1934.
- Hitler aimed to create a Greater German empire, with the conquest of eastern Europe and the destruction of the *USSR*. He was chiefly responsible for the outbreak of the Second World War in Europe (1939), through annexation of Austria (the *Anschluss*), the *Sudetenland*, and finally his attack on Poland.
- Having blamed Germany's defeat in the First World War, and its subsequent economic difficulties, on an international Jewish conspiracy, and propagating a belief in the innate superiority of the Aryan race, he launched the *Final Solution* to exterminate Europe's Jews and gypsies.
- After rapidly conquering Poland, France, Norway, the Low Countries and much of Russia, he was finally defeated in war by the Grand Alliance of Britain, the USA and the USSR.
- Having survived an assassination attempt in the *July Plot* (1944), he committed suicide in April 1945 as Russian soldiers entered Berlin.

▓ *TIP* Hitler was a key European figure in the 1930s and a major cause of the Second World War. With the possible exception of *Stalin*, he was the most ruthless dictator of the twentieth century.

Hitler Youth: a Nazi organisation for boys aged 14–18.

- Similar to the Scout movement, but with strong political indoctrination, the Hitler Youth was part of an overall Nazi programme to control its citizens.
- In the Second World War it provided troops for the Twelfth *SS* Panzer (Hitler Youth) Division.

▓ *TIP* The organisation was part of a Nazi plan for *Volksgemeinschaft* (folk community).

Hoare–Laval Pact, 1935: an attempt to *appease Mussolini*, made by the foreign ministers of Britain and France.

- The pact offered to accept a substantial Italian presence in Abyssinia (Ethiopia), following the Italian invasion.
- The proposal met with a hostile reception in both Britain and France and was never accepted by either government.

h

■ *TIP* This pact was an early example of the policy of appeasement, made on behalf of Britain and France.

Ho Chi Minh: Vietnamese communist leader, who declared Vietnam independent in 1954 and led the *Vietminh* in a war against the French (1946–54).

● He founded the Vietminh organisation for the purpose of liberating Vietnam from French and Japanese control in 1941.

● He became the first head of state of communist North Vietnam, later organising communist attacks on South Vietnam.

■ *TIP* He was a crucial figure in the creation of an independent Vietnam.

Holocaust: see *Final Solution*.

Holy Alliance, 1815–55: an international agreement between European monarchs.

● It was first suggested by Tsar *Alexander I*, in an attempt to stem the tide of liberalism, and became the chief bulwark of autocratic monarchy.

● The three Eastern *Great Powers* of Russia, Austria and Prussia worked together to achieve this aim. They suppressed the Polish Revolt of 1830–31 and re-affirmed their commitment to the alliance at the *Münchengratz* meeting of 1833.

● In 1849 Russian troops helped Austria to suppress the Hungarian Revolution.

● The alliance came to an end when Austria supported Britain and France in the *Crimean War*.

■ *TIP* The Holy Alliance is important in explaining international stability in Europe between 1815 and 1854. Once it collapsed, Austria had to fight France alone in 1859, and Prussia alone in 1866. Both wars transformed Europe, helping to create the unification of Italy and Germany respectively.

Hoover, Herbert: US President (1929–33), whose term of office was over-shadowed by the Depression caused by the *Wall Street Crash*.

● His belief in the importance of laissez-faire (free-market) economics made it difficult for Hoover to use federal power to help with the Depression.

● However, in 1932 he set up the *Reconstruction Finance Corporation*, which offered federal help to businesses. Hoover also cancelled certain debt repayments, which led to the cancellation of reparations by Germany.

■ *TIP* Hoover's failure to get the USA out of depression was the result of a decade of Republican free-market economic policies. It took F. D. *Roosevelt* and the *New Deal* to begin a recovery.

Hoover, J. Edgar: Head of the Federal Bureau of Investigation (FBI), 1924–72.

● He reorganised the FBI in the 1930s, concentrating its efforts on fighting gangsters.

● From the 1940s onwards the FBI was used to investigate spies and communist sympathisers in the USA.

● By the 1960s the FBI was very powerful and began investigating Black *civil rights* leaders and members of the government.

■ *TIP* The FBI under Hoover became the major federal law enforcement agency. Hoover used its powers against his political opponents.

Hossbach Memorandum, 1937: a report of a meeting between *Hitler* and his senior military staff and foreign ministry, in which he outlined his plan to go to war by 1943 to create 'living space' (*Lebensraum*) for the German people in eastern Europe.

- The memorandum has been seen by some historians as a blueprint for war. Others (like William Carr) link the meeting to a dispute between *Goering* and Blomberg (the Minister of War) over the pace of rearmament.
- It could also be seen as a prelude to the *Blomberg–Fritsch Affair* in 1938, when Hitler took personal command of the armed forces.
- *TIP* The Hossbach Memorandum is important evidence in any study of Hitler's planning for the Second World War.

Hugenburg, Alfred: leader of the German National People's Party in *Weimar* Germany.

- He was an opponent of democracy and led a right-wing campaign against accepting the *Young Plan* of 1929.
- He controlled several newspapers, which were used in his campaigns. In allowing the Nazis to join the anti-Young Plan campaign, he helped increase Nazi popularity.
- He was one of *Hindenburg*'s advisers, who persuaded him to appoint Hitler as Chancellor in 1933.
- *TIP* Hugenburg led the largest conservative, anti-democratic party in Weimar Germany. He helped pave the way for increased electoral support for the Nazis in the 1930 *Reichstag* elections.

Hungarian Uprising, 1956: an attempt by Hungarian nationalists to overthrow the communist regime, which was crushed by a Soviet invasion.

- The uprising was prompted by the *destalinisation* speech made by *Khrushchev*.
- It was led by Imre Nagy; the Hungarian rebels declared a free press, multi-party elections and withdrawal from the *Warsaw Pact*.
- When the Soviet Union sent in tanks, the USA and other Western powers did not intervene.
- *TIP* The Hungarian Uprising showed up the limited support for communism in eastern Europe. Communist governments were kept in power by force.

hyperinflation: a period of rapidly rising prices, in which monetary denominations quickly lose their value.

- It affected *Weimar* Germany between 1922 and 1924. It also plagued Germany and Hungary immediately after the Second World War.
- In Weimar Germany hyperinflation came to an end with the introduction of a new currency, the *Rentenmark*, which was backed by the Rentenbank mortgaging all German land and industry.
- *TIP* Hyperinflation in Weimar Germany wiped out middle-class savings, making the German economy over-dependent on foreign loans for investment.

ICBM: see *intercontinental ballistic missile*.

immigration quotas: introduced in the USA in the early 1920s, as their first restriction on immigration.

- In 1921 *Congress* passed the Emergency Immigration Act, which imposed an annual quota on immigration from Europe.
- The quota was based on the proportion of nationals from that country living in the USA in 1911, which favoured northern and western European immigrants.
- In 1924 the Johnson-Reed Immigration Act banned immigration from Japan.
- **TIP** The quota system was part of a reaction of White, Anglo-Saxon Protestants (WASPS) to social developments in the USA. It should be considered along with *Prohibition*, the reappearance of the *Ku Klux Klan* and opposition to socialism.

Independent Social Democrats (USPD): a German political party (1917–24), which split from the rest of the *Social Democrat Party* (SPD), which then became known as the 'Majority Social Democrats'.

- The main reason for the split was a difference in opinion over how to end the war, not differences in political ideas. The USPD strongly supported the Peace Resolution of 1917. It joined with the SPD in November 1918 in the first revolutionary government of Germany.
- It split again from the SPD, following the government's suppression of the *Spartacist* (communist) *Uprising* of January 1919. It won 22 seats in the 1919 *Reichstag* elections, and 84 seats in 1920. Thereafter, the party went into rapid decline.
- **TIP** The breakaway of the USPD was an important development in the division of German socialists, which increased political instability in *Weimar* Germany in its early years.

INF: see *intermediate nuclear forces*.

intercontinental ballistic missile (ICBM): a long-range nuclear weapon, developed by both the USA and the *USSR* during the 1950s.

- The ICBM became the mainstay of the superpowers' nuclear arsenals from the 1960s onwards. Both sides faced 'mutually assured destruction' (MAD) as a result. By the late 1960s, however, both sides had developed an anti-ballistic missile (ABM) system.

- The *Strategic Arms Limitation* talks between the USA and the USSR resulted in the SALT I Treaty (1972), which limited the number of ABMs. The SALT II Treaty (1979) placed an upper limit on ICBMs.

■ *TIP* The nuclear arms race was central to the *Cold War* conflict between the superpowers and highlighted the need by both sides to negotiate limits on their development.

intermediate nuclear forces (INF): nuclear weapons to be used within a continent, rather than between continents, which became the focus for superpower talks in the 1980s.

- The *USSR* deployed the SS20 missile, while the Americans deployed the Pershing II and Cruise missiles in Europe.
- These weapons led to a major increase in *Cold War* tension. Talks began in 1985 and a treaty was signed between *Reagan* and *Gorbachev* in 1987, which aimed to eliminate all INF forces from Europe within 3 years.

■ *TIP* The INF Treaty was the first genuine attempt to reduce nuclear arsenals, although it applied to only 4% of nuclear weapons.

Iranian Revolution, 1979: the overthrow of the Shah of Iran by Muslim traditionalists.

- The Shah (Emperor) of Iran was a pro-Western dictator. In November 1978 a general revolt against his rule began. He left the country, to be replaced by the Muslim religious leader Ayatollah *Khomeini*, who returned to Iran from exile.
- Iran was transformed into a traditional Muslim society, with strong anti-Western views. Between 1979 and 1981 the Iranians held the staff of the US embassy in Iran hostage.

■ *TIP* The Iranian Revolution was an important episode in the rise of traditional Islamic views, which has affected the Middle East and North Africa from 1979 to the present day.

Iran–Iraq War, 1980–88: a major Middle Eastern conflict, which arose out of the *Iranian Revolution* of 1979.

- Political disarray in Iran encouraged the Iraqi leader, Saddam Hussein, to seize oil-rich Iranian territory near the Persian Gulf.
- The longest conventional war of the twentieth century ensued. Neither side was able to win a decisive victory. The war cost 1 million lives and left the Iran–Iraq border in virtually the same place as it was in 1980.

■ *TIP* The war helped strengthen Ayatollah *Khomeini*'s control over Iran. It forced Saddam Hussein to search for other oil-rich territory to conquer, leading directly to the invasion of Kuwait in 1991.

Iron Curtain: a term used to describe the division between the communist and non-communist world in Europe after the Second World War.

- The term was first used by Josef *Goebbels*, but most famously by Winston *Churchill* at Fulton, Missouri, in 1946.

- Churchill claimed that communist control of eastern Europe had created a separate zone of dictatorship. He called for Western vigilance when dealing with the *USSR*.

■ *TIP* As a result of Churchill's important speech, relations between East and West deteriorated. President *Truman* was present at the speech, signifying unity between Britain and the USA against the USSR.

Jacobins: a radical French revolutionary group, also known as the 'Friends of the Constitution'.

● Formed as a club in 1789, the Jacobins were leading supporters of the creation of a republic and the rule of the *Committee of Public Safety*, led by *Robespierre*.

● They lost influence with the fall of Robespierre in 1795.

▧ *TIP* Remember that the French Revolution produced a number of rival political groups. Ensure that you use the terms correctly.

jacquerie: a spontaneous peasant uprising, in response to conditions of distress.

● They usually occurred in periods of famine, or near famine. Peasants often attacked millers, whom they habitually accused of storing grain. They also attacked landowners, to destroy records of payment on land.

● Although violent, *jacqueries* generally lasted a relatively short period of time. They occurred during the French Revolution, during the revolutions of 1848, and in Russia in the late-nineteenth and early-twentieth centuries.

▧ *TIP* Use the term accurately. Several types of popular uprising occurred in the wake of the French Revolution. *Jacqueries* were reactive, lacked clear leadership and usually failed to bring any lasting change.

Jameson Raid, 1895–96: an attempt to overthrow the government of the Transvaal in South Africa by British mercenaries.

● Organised by the Prime Minister of Cape Colony, Cecil Rhodes, the Jameson Raid was intended to assist an uprising against the Boer government in the goldfields of the Transvaal. Rhodes hoped to turn the Transvaal into a British colony.

● The raid backfired when no uprising occurred and its leader, Jameson, was captured by the Transvaalers.

● The Colonial Secretary, Joseph Chamberlain, was implicated in the plan but was exonerated.

▧ *TIP* The raid was an important cause of the *Boer War*. It convinced the Transvaal government that Britain intended to take over their country.

Jim Crow Laws: a term given to racist laws passed in the Southern States, following reconstruction after the American Civil War.

● The aim was to prevent African Americans from voting. The laws included the 'grandfather clause', which stated that if your grandfather could not vote, you had no right to vote. Literacy tests, poll taxes and all-White primary elections also excluded the majority of African Americans from the political process.

- The laws were further intended to segregate Southern society between Whites and African Americans.
- ■ *TIP* The laws were central to the recapture of state and local government in the Old South by Whites, in the years following 1877.

Johnson, Lyndon: US President (1963–69), who tackled the issue of poverty in his 'Great Society' programme of social reforms.

- He took office following the assassination of John *Kennedy*.
- In addition to social reform, President Johnson initiated the *Civil Rights Act* of 1964, the Voting Rights Act of 1965 and the Poll Tax amendment to the Constitution, giving African Americans political and civil equality.
- He also escalated US involvement in the *Vietnam War*, by committing American ground troops in 1965. By the end of his presidency the US had 600,000 troops in South Vietnam.
- ■ *TIP* Johnson's administration was one of the most important since *Roosevelt's*, but military expenditure on Vietnam undermined his social programmes. He was the last president to use federal power so widely in domestic affairs.

Johnson Doctrine, 1965: a declaration by President *Johnson* that the American nations could not, and would not, permit the establishment of another communist government in the western hemisphere.

- The Doctrine was used to intervene in the Dominican Republic in 1965, when a socialist government took power.
- It was called into question in 1970, when an extreme left-wing government was elected in Chile under Salvador Allende.
- ■ *TIP* It was part of a US policy which attempted to isolate Cuba.

July Crisis, 1914: a political crisis which resulted in the outbreak of the First World War. It began with the assassination, by a Bosnian Serb, of the Austrian Archduke Franz Ferdinand in *Sarajevo*.

- As a result of the assassination Austria-Hungary declared war on Serbia, with German backing.
- The crisis developed into a European war, partly because statesmen had to make decisions quickly in order to mobilise their armies.
- Germany activated the *Schlieffen Plan* and attacked Belgium, which brought Britain into the war.
- ■ *TIP* The July Crisis highlighted the problems associated with dividing Europe into two armed camps: the *Triple Alliance* and the Franco–Russian Alliance.

July Days, Russia, 1917: an attempt by *Lenin* and the *Bolsheviks* to gain political power through street demonstrations.

- On his return to Russia in 1917, Lenin advocated a Bolshevik seizure of power. He used the failure of the Russian July Offensive in an attempt to force the *Provisional Government* to resign.

- Instead, the Russian leader, Alexander *Kerensky*, suppressed the demonstrations. Lenin fled to Finland.
- Only after the *Kornilov Affair* did Lenin attempt another seizure of power.
- **TIP** The events of the July Days show that not all Lenin's tactics worked. In exile Lenin wrote ***The State and Revolution***, which suggested that the Bolsheviks might not take power during his lifetime.

July Plot, 1944: an attempt to assassinate *Hitler*, with a bomb left in a briefcase.

- Codenamed Operation Valkyrie, the plot was hatched by senior members of the German armed forces, who hoped to assassinate Hitler in the 'Wolf's Lair', his headquarters in East Prussia. The conspirators then hoped to negotiate an end to the war.
- The plot failed. Hitler was only slightly hurt, although several members of his staff were killed or wounded.
- The failure led to a purge of the Army and the trial and execution of participants.
- **TIP** This was the most serious attempt to assassinate Hitler and it ended his respect for the Army leadership. He later appointed Admiral *Doenitz* as his successor.

July Revolution, France, 1830: led to the overthrow of the Bourbon monarchy in France and its replacement with the Orleans monarchy.

- It was sparked off by the *Ordinances of St Cloud*, whereby *Charles X* attempted to increase his political power.
- The Ordinances led to 3 days of rioting in Paris. Failure to quell the riots was due partly to Charles X's decision to abolish the National Guard in 1827, and to his use of the Army to conquer Algiers.
- The new monarch, *Louis Philippe*, had royal blood, but also had links to the French Revolution through his father. Known as the 'Citizen King', Louis Philippe ruled until 1848.
- **TIP** The July Revolution, like 1789 and 1848, was centred on Paris. It was also unplanned.

June Days of 1848: rioting in Paris, brought about by the government decision to end unemployment relief (the *National Workshops*).

- The rioters were mainly craftsmen, who had suffered badly during industrialisation. They attempted to create a socialist republic.
- The uprising was put down by General Cavaignac, but led to the development of a moderate *Second French Republic.*
- **TIP** The June Days is an example of a split in the revolutionaries, who brought down *Louis Philippe*, between moderate and radical. Such splits also occurred following the *July Revolution* of 1830 and in the revolutions in Germany in 1848–49.

Junker: a Prussian landowner, usually with lands east of the River Elbe.

- The Junkers dominated Prussian politics until the mid-twentieth century. *Bismarck* was a junker.

- Junkers maintained political power through the 'three-class suffrage' of 1848–1918, which guaranteed them one-third of the seats in the Prussian *Landtag* (parliament).
- During the *Second Reich* (1871–1918), Junkers feared economic ruin from the importation of cheap Russian grain. They pressured the government to introduce tariffs and supported an anti-Russian foreign policy. In 1893 they helped to establish the *Bund der Landwirte* (Agrarian League) to defend their interests.

TIP The term Junker can be used to describe the politically conservative, landowner class in either Prussia or the German empire.

Kadet: a member of the Russian Constitutional Democrat Party.

- Founded at the beginning of the twentieth century, the Kadets regarded the *October Manifesto* of 1905 as the beginning of political reform in Russia.
- Under the leadership of Paul Miliukov the Kadets won 182 of the 448 seats in the first *Duma*, but their support declined in the subsequent Dumas before the outbreak of war in 1914.
- During the war the Kadets formed part of the progressive bloc of centre and leftist parties, which wanted further reform.
- Following the *February Revolution*, the Kadets were major supporters of the *Provisional Government*. However, in the Constituent Assembly elections in December 1917 their support dropped dramatically.
- *TIP* The Kadets were one half of the liberal grouping in the Duma, along with the *Octobrists*. Party support was mainly limited to the middle classes living in towns.

Kamenev, Lev: a Russian communist leader, who opposed the *Bolshevik* seizure of power in October 1917 but became *Lenin*'s deputy and leader of the *Petrograd* Party.

- Following Lenin's death, Kamenev sided with *Zinoviev* and *Stalin* against *Trotsky*.
- He was subsequently ousted from power by Stalin in 1926. In 1935 he was put on trial with Zinoviev and 17 others for plotting Kirov's death. He was sentenced to death.
- *TIP* Kamenev was an important Russian communist who assisted Stalin's rise to power, but was murdered in the Great *Purge* of the mid-1930s.

Kapp Putsch, 1920: an attempt to overthrow the democratic government of the *Weimar Republic* by right-wing nationalists, assisted by the *Freikorps*.

- Its leader, Kapp, had been a member of the right-wing Fatherland Front Party in the closing stages of the First World War.
- The attempt failed, because the trade unions organised a general strike.
- *TIP* The Kapp Putsch is a good example of how supporters of the previous imperial regime attempted to regain power.

Kellogg–Briand Pact, 1928: an international agreement, which sought to renounce war as a method of settling disputes.

- It was initially signed by the USA, Britain, France, Germany, Italy and Japan.
- ■ *TIP* Along with the *Geneva Protocol* of 1924 and the *Locarno Treaties* of 1925, this pact suggested a move towards maintaining world peace. However, the onset of the Depression brought to an end a period of optimism. In 1931 one of the signatories, Japan, invaded Manchuria in northern China.

Kemal Atatürk (Mustafa Kemal)**:** the founder of modern Turkey.

- A member of the *Young Turk* movement in the Army in 1908, he helped to defend the Gallipoli peninsula from Allied attack in 1915.
- He was involved in the overthrow of the Sultan in 1920, after which he set up a provisional government for a Turkish Republic.
- He led the Turks to victory in the Graeco–Turkish War of 1920–23, which won back territory lost in the Treaty of *Sèvres*.
- In the 1920s he created social and political revolution in Turkey. He limited the power and influence of Islam, introduced a new Western alphabet and westernised Turkish dress. He brought about a great change in the social position of Turkish women.
- ■ *TIP* Ataturk was a great modernising statesman, following the collapse of the *Ottoman empire*.

Kennedy, John F.: US President (1961–63), whose short term in office, curtailed by his assassination in Dallas, involved two major superpower clashes: the *Berlin Wall Crisis* (1961) and the *Cuban Missile Crisis* (1962).

- A believer in the *domino theory*, he sent military advisers to South Vietnam and financed a covert war, directed by the *CIA*, against communism in Laos.
- In domestic affairs, he faced a hostile conservative coalition in *Congress* between Republicans and Southern Democrats, which all but destroyed his *New Frontier* programme.
- He was forced to take action to defend African Americans who wished to desegregate university education and interstate busing in the Old South.
- ■ *TIP* Kennedy's presidency is central to any study of US involvement in Southeast Asia.

Kent State shootings, 1970: the occasion when four students from Kent State University were shot by National Guardsmen, during a protest against the US invasion of Cambodia.

- This was the worst incident in a wave of violent unrest following President *Nixon*'s decision to escalate the *Vietnam War* by invading neutral Cambodia.
- ■ *TIP* The antiwar movement was a major factor in forcing the US government to seek an end to the Vietnam War. Nixon's invasion of Cambodia was part of his policy to secure 'peace with honour'.

Kerensky, Alexander: a Russian politician and leader of the *Provisional Government* from July to October 1917.

- A member of the *Duma*, he was the only socialist in the first Provisional Government (February–July 1917).

- Initially a popular figure, Kerensky lost support through continuing Russia's involvement in the First World War.
- He mishandled the *Kornilov Affair*, which undermined his government. This made it easier for the *Bolsheviks* to seize power in October 1917.
- ■ *TIP* Kerensky's career mirrored the failings of the Provisional Government and showed why it lasted for such a short time.

KGB (Committee of State Security): Soviet Secret Police (1954–91), successor to the *Cheka, OGPU* and *NKVD*.

- Created following the execution of *Beria*, the Secret Police was brought under the direct control of the Communist Party. Each republic had a KGB head.
- It was active not just in the *USSR*, but in the rest of the world. Beyond the *Iron Curtain*, the KGB was involved in espionage and support for pro-Soviet groups.
- The most significant head of the KGB was Yuri *Andropov* (1967–82). He left to become Soviet leader on the death of *Brezhnev*.

Khomeini, Ayatollah: a religious and political leader who instigated the *Iranian Revolution* against the Shah (Emperor) of Iran in 1979. He created a fundamentalist, anti-Western Islamic state. This involved the imprisonment as hostages of US embassy staff in Iran from 1979 to 1981. He led Iran through the *Iran–Iraq War* of 1980–88, but died before a cease-fire was created.

- ■ *TIP* Ayatollah Khomeini is a representative of the growth of anti-Western Islamic feeling which has developed across the Muslim world since the 1970s. Islamic states, such as Iran and Libya, have partly replaced the *USSR* and its satellites as the USA's main opposition throughout the world.

Khrushchev, Nikita: Soviet leader (1955–64), who introduced domestic reforms, reduced the *Gulag* concentration camp system and attempted to reform Soviet agriculture.

- He denounced *Stalin* at the Twentieth Congress of the Soviet Communist Party in 1956.
- In foreign affairs, he attempted to force the Western powers out of Berlin. This led to the *Berlin Wall Crisis* (1961). His most serious misjudgement, in placing Soviet missiles on Cuba, led to the *Cuban Missile Crisis* (1962).
- Failures at home and abroad led to his dismissal in 1964.
- ■ *TIP* Khrushchev ruled during one of the most tense periods of the *Cold War*.

Kiel Mutiny, 1918: took place when the German High Seas Fleet was ordered to attack the British Navy. Defying orders, the men set up sailors' councils — similar to *soviets* in Russia. The mutiny sparked off the German Revolution of October/November 1918.

- Unrest spread through the German armed forces and civilian population, forcing the Kaiser to abdicate.
- ■ *TIP* The Kiel Mutiny was unplanned, but it acted as a catalyst to spark unrest across Germany.

King, Martin Luther: African American *civil rights* leader, who believed in non-violent protest.

- He became leader of the Southern Christian Leadership Conference in 1956, and thus unofficial leader of the Black civil rights movement. He led marches and demonstrations against segregation, which won him the Nobel Peace Prize in 1964.
- He came to criticise US involvement in the *Vietnam War* after 1967. He was assassinated in 1968.
- **TIP** King played an important role in the civil rights movement. Successful in reducing discrimination in the South, he was less successful in the North. Recently, historians have downplayed his influence on the movement.

Kissinger, Henry: US foreign affairs specialist, who was National Security Adviser (1969–73) and Secretary of State (1973–77).

- Known for his 'shuttle diplomacy', he negotiated *détente* with the *USSR* in 1971 and helped to restore US relations with communist China in 1972.
- He negotiated the Vietnam Peace Agreement of 1973, for which he received a Nobel Peace Prize.
- He also helped to bring the *Yom Kippur War* to an end.
- **TIP** Kissinger was a major influence on US foreign policy under both *Nixon* and *Ford*.

Kleindeutschland: a 'little Germany' solution to the problem of German unification, which proposed exclusion of the Austrian empire from a united Germany, leaving Prussia as the dominant state.

- This solution was accepted by the *Frankfurt Parliament* in 1849, but the King of Prussia rejected the offer of the German crown.
- **TIP** The contrasting *Kleindeutschland* and *Grossdeutschland* proposals became a central issue in the debate on German unification in the mid-nineteenth century.

kolkhoz: a Soviet collective farm.

- *Kolkhoz* were set up during the forced collectivisation of Soviet agriculture from 1928 onwards. Private farms were abolished. All machinery and livestock were to be owned jointly by members of the collective farm.
- *Sovkhoz* were collective farms owned directly by the Soviet government.
- **TIP** Collectivisation had disastrous consequences for Soviet agriculture, from which it has never fully recovered. Production fell and over 5 million died in the famine of 1932–33.

Korean War, 1950–53: the first major armed conflict of the *Cold War*.

- It began with the invasion of South Korea by communist North Korea in June 1950.
- President *Truman* decided that the USA should intervene militarily, in support of the *United Nations*. The USA was supported by other UN members, such as Britain and France.
- By 1951 the war had reached a stalemate close to the original borders of North and South Korea. A cease-fire took place in 1953.
- **TIP** The Korean War is a good example of the success of the US policy of *containment* of communism in Asia.

Kornilov Affair, 1917: an episode which undermined the Russian *Provisional Government* and allowed the *Bolsheviks* to regain popularity.

- The commander of the Russian Army, Lev Kornilov, sent troops to *Petrograd* to control left-wing agitators.
- *Kerensky*, the leader of the government, believed Kornilov was planning a military take-over. He panicked and gave weapons to socialist workers, including Bolsheviks. Kornilov was relieved of his command.

▓ *TIP* This incident was an important step in the decline of the Provisional Government and the rise of the Bolsheviks.

Kossuth, Louis: a nationalist leader, who led the 1848–49 Hungarian Revolution against the Habsburgs.

- He first rose to prominence in the Hungarian Diet (assembly), where he suggested that Hungary should embrace parliamentary government.
- He helped to abolish the ***Robot*** (feudal obligations by peasants to landlords) and made Magyar the official language of Hungary.
- He split away from more moderate Hungarians in 1849, when he declared an independent Hungarian republic. This was crushed by Austrian and Russian armies.

▓ *TIP* Kossuth in 1848 was a fine example of a liberal, nationalist revolutionary. However, his radicalism divided the Hungarian nationalist movement.

Kraft durch Freude: the 'Strength through Joy' movement, which organised leisure facilities for the German population under the Nazis.

- It was created in 1933 as part of the German Labour Front and ran holiday camps and provided Mediterranean and Atlantic cruises.
- It also administered the system whereby ordinary Germans could purchase a Volkswagen ('people's car').

▓ *TIP* The movement was an important part of the Nazi plan for *Volksgemeinschaft* (folk community).

***Kristallnacht*, 1938:** the 'Night of Breaking Glass', which was a key event in the Nazi persecution of the Jews.

- Following the assassination of a German diplomat in Paris by a Polish Jew, *SS* leader Reinhard *Heydrich* organised the mass destruction of synagogues and Jewish-owned buildings.
- Over 100 Jews were murdered and several thousand were sent to concentration camps.

▓ *TIP* *Kristallnacht* was the worst case of persecution against the Jews before the outbreak of the Second World War. It supports the view of some historians that the *Final Solution* had become Nazi policy even before the war.

Kronstadt Mutiny, 1921: a rising by sailors of the Revolutionary Baltic Fleet against *Lenin*'s communist government.

- Left-wing revolutionaries in the fleet had become disillusioned with Lenin's terror tactics and control of the economy.
- The rising was put down by the *Red Army* under the personal direction of *Trotsky*.

- The mutiny helped to push Lenin towards reform at the Tenth Party Congress in 1921, where he abandoned *war communism* in favour of the *New Economic Policy*.
- It was also regarded as the last battle of the Russian Civil War.
- **TIP** The mutiny showed that Lenin was a practical, realistic politician. He introduced the more moderate New Economic Policy. The event also led to a ban on factions and the introduction of democratic centralism in the Communist Party.

Ku Klux Klan: a White supremacist organisation which spread throughout the USA. It was anti-Black, anti-Catholic and anti-Semitic.

- Formed in 1866, it initially opposed the Reconstruction policies of the federal government following the Civil War. The original Klan was disbanded in 1870.
- It was revived in 1915 and became a nationwide secret society, but it went into marked decline after 1925, when one of its leaders was arrested for attempted rape.
- **TIP** The Ku Klux Klan and other secret societies were important defenders of White supremacist governments in the Old South.

kulak: a rich peasant in Russia/*USSR*.

- Following *Stolypin*'s reforms (1907–11), some peasants became outright owners of their land. Some employed other peasants as labourers.
- Communists regarded *kulaks* as counter-revolutionary. *Stalin* planned to destroy the *kulak* class during the process of forced *collectivisation* after 1928.
- The term came to be used to describe anyone who opposed collectivisation. Even poor peasants were accused of having a *kulak* mentality.
- Collectivisation succeeded in destroying the *kulaks*.
- **TIP** This is an important term in understanding the problems that the communist revolutionaries had in introducing their political and social system into Russia. *Lenin* created a republic of workers and peasants in 1917. It took Stalin, from 1928 onwards, to bring a social revolution to the USSR by destroying the Russian peasant class.

Kulturkampf: the 'culture struggle' — anti-Catholic policies of *Bismarck*'s government from 1872 to 1885.

- Following the creation of the German empire in 1871, Bismarck feared *Reichsfeinde* (groups which might undermine German unity).
- He attacked the Catholics because of their links with Polish nationalism in eastern Prussia. His attack would also win support from the *National Liberals*, Bismarck's main supporters in the *Reichstag*. Religious orders were banned and priests became paid government employees.
- *Kulturkampf* backfired and helped the growth of the Catholic *Centre Party*. By 1878 Bismarck needed Centre Party support to introduce tariffs, so he relaxed the anti-Catholic laws, which finally came to an end in 1885.
- **TIP** *Kulturkampf* is a fine example of Bismarck's fear of threats to a Prussian-dominated Germany.

Kuomintang: the Chinese Nationalist Party, founded by Sun Yat Sen.

- It established a Chinese Republic in 1911, coming under the leadership of *Chiang Kai Shek* in the 1920s.
- It launched a civil war against the Chinese communists, which lasted until the communist victory in 1949.
- The Kuomintang retreated to the island of Taiwan (which it refers to as the Republic of China) and has since dominated its politics.

■ *TIP* Conflict between Chinese nationalists and communists has been a major feature of east Asian relations since the 1920s. In the second half of the twentieth century the USA intervened several times to prevent war between the two sides.

Kursk, Battle of, 1943: a major battle on the Eastern Front, which turned out to be the last German *blitzkrieg* attack in the East.

- It was repulsed by the *Red Army* in the greatest tank battle in history, involving over 5,000 vehicles.

■ *TIP* This battle, rather than *Stalingrad*, was the real turning-point on the Eastern Front. After Kursk, the Red Army knew only victories, the Germans only defeats.

levée en masse: a form of compulsory military service introduced by the *Committee of Public Safety* in 1793, during the French Revolution.

- It enabled the Revolutionary government to raise large armies — which *Napoleon* subsequently used to conquer much of Europe.
- *TIP* This policy helps to explain why the French Revolutionary and Napoleonic armies were so successful.

Leyte Gulf, Battle of, 1944: a major US naval victory over the Japanese, prior to the invasion of the Philippines.

- The battle was dominated by aircraft carriers; neither side came into visual contact.
- It was the biggest naval engagement in history, in which the US Third and Seventh fleets destroyed Japanese naval and air power in the Pacific. It cleared the way for an invasion of the Philippines.
- *TIP* The battle can be regarded as the beginning of the end of the Pacific War against Japan.

Lloyd George, David: Prime Minister (1916–22), who led Britain to victory in the First World War.

- Prior to the First World War Lloyd George was a radical Liberal and was responsible for introducing old age pensions, progressive taxation and reform of the House of Lords.
- He was a successful Minister of Munitions (1915–16) and, on becoming Prime Minister, reorganised Cabinet government and the war effort to ensure victory.
- At the *Paris Peace* Conference (1919–20) his fear of the spread of communism helped to moderate his views towards Germany. He adopted a position between the leniency of the USA and France, which wanted to punish Germany while leaving the German state intact.
- After the war he signed a treaty with the Irish Republican Party, Sinn Fein, which created the Irish Free State (1922).
- *TIP* He played an important part in securing British successes in the First World War.

Locarno, Treaty of, 1925: an international agreement whereby Germany accepted the territorial changes made by the Treaty of *Versailles* (1919).

- The German Foreign Minister, *Stresemann*, accepted Germany's new borders with Belgium and France, but not its new eastern borders.
- As a result Germany was allowed to join the *League of Nations* in 1926.
- *TIP* This was an important, if ultimately unsuccessful, development in creating stability in postwar Europe. *Hitler* broke the treaty when he remilitarised the Rhineland in 1936.

Long Telegram, 1946: the first major statement putting forward the US policy of *containment* of the *USSR*.

- The telegram was compiled by the US Ambassador to the USSR, George Kennan.

- It postulated that the only diplomacy *Stalin* would heed would be backed by military force.
- This became the basis of the *Truman Doctrine* (1947).
- ■ *TIP* The Long Telegram was an important development in the deterioration of relations between the USA and USSR after 1945. It showed that the USA, as well as the USSR, was responsible for this deterioration.

Louis XVI: King of France (1774–93), who precipitated the French Revolution by taking France into bankruptcy.

- French intervention in the American War of Independence (1776–83) put a financial strain on the country which successive finance ministers, such as Turgot and Calonne, could not overcome.
- France became bankrupt in 1787. This forced Louis to call the *Estates General* (1789) to deal with the financial crisis.
- The decision of the 'Third Estate' to meet separately as the National Assembly sparked off the Revolution.
- Louis XVI's reluctance to accept any diminution in his political power, and his links with foreign powers such as Austria and Prussia, led to his trial and execution by the National Convention (1793).
- ■ *TIP* Louis's character and personality were important factors in the causes and development of the French Revolution.

Louis XVIII: King of France (1814 and 1815–24) and member of the Bourbon family, who was restored to the throne by the Allies following the defeat of *Napoleon*.

- He accepted the *Charter* as the constitution of France and ruled as a constitutional monarch.
- Following his death, *Charles X* established a more conservative regime.
- ■ *TIP* Louis XVIII was unable to prevent the rise of the *Ultras*, the conservative monarchists who supported Charles X.

Louis Philippe: King of France (1830–48), who came to the throne as the 'Citizen King' in the *July Revolution*, following the overthrow of *Charles X*.

- His popularity gradually waned, as his successive governments failed to introduce political and social reforms.
- After 1840 he was closely identified with *Guizot*. When Guizot was forced to resign as Prime Minister in 1848, Louis Philippe fled to England.
- ■ *TIP* Louis Philippe's reign was one of a succession of attempts to establish a stable regime following the Revolution and the Napoleonic empire. However, it took until the Third Republic (1870) for a system of government to emerge in France which was not hopelessly divisive.

Ludendorff, Erich von: a leading German general in the First World War, who intrigued with *Hitler* in the *Beer Hall Putsch* (1923) to overthrow the government of the *Weimar Republic*.

- He led the assault on Liège during the German attack on the West in August 1914. He was then moved to the Eastern Front with von *Hindenburg*, where he defeated the Russian Army at *Tannenberg* (1914).

- In 1916 he was instrumental in the overthrow of Chancellor *Bethmann-Hollweg* and the rise in political influence of the Army High Command. With Hindenburg, he led the *March Offensive* on the Western Front in 1918.
- Following his involvement with the Beer Hall Putsch he was put on trial, but was acquitted.

■ *TIP* Ludendorff was an important figure in the rise of military influence over the German government during the First World War.

Lunch Counter Protests, 1960: African American protests against segregation of lunch counters.

- Organised by the Student Non-Violent Coordinating Committee, the protests began in a Woolworths store in North Carolina and spread across the Old South.
- This was a successful case of direct action, which achieved desegregation.

■ *TIP* The protests ended the dominance of the South Christian Leadership Conference in the Black *civil rights* movement.

Luxemburg, Rosa: leader of the *Spartacists* and co-founder of the German Communist Party.

- A Polish Jew and founder of the Polish Social Democrat Party in Switzerland, she took part in the Russian *Revolution of 1905*.
- With Karl Liebknecht, she founded the German Spartacist League and, in 1918, the German Communist Party. Centrally involved in the Spartacist Uprising in Berlin in 1919, she was captured and murdered by the *Freikorps*.

■ *TIP* Rosa Luxemburg was a leading figure in the attempt to establish communism in Germany at the end of the First World War.

Maastricht, Treaty of, 1991: an agreement to introduce a single currency and improved workers' rights into the *European Economic Community*, which also changed its name to the *European Union*.

- The treaty also provided for increased powers for the European Parliament.
- The Danes voted against the treaty in a referendum. Britain signed up to it, but without agreeing to the 'Social Chapter' on workers' rights.

▨ *TIP* The treaty was an important landmark in the development of the EU, emphasising closer economic and political integration.

McCarthy, Joseph: a Republican Senator who led anti-communist witch-hunts in the USA between 1947 and 1954.

- Using the Congressional Committee on Unamerican Activities, he sought to uncover communists and communist sympathisers. His activities helped to undermine *Truman*'s (Democrat) administration.
- McCarthy was criticised in 1954 for claiming that communists had infiltrated the armed forces. His influence declined rapidly.

▨ *TIP* 'McCarthyism' was used as a political weapon by the Republicans to attack the Democrats (1947–53). His activities show the degree of anti-communist feeling there was in the USA.

Maginot Line: French defensive fortifications, built in the 1930s along the Franco–German border.

- Based on the experience of the First World War, its aim was to make the frontier impregnable to German attack. A plan to extend the line to the Belgian border was never realised.
- In 1940 the line was outflanked by a German *blitzkrieg* attack through Belgium.

▨ *TIP* The line gave France a false sense of security and helped prevent French action against remilitarisation of the Rhineland in 1936. It also prevented the creation of a French mobile reserve in 1940.

mandates: the system set up by the *Paris Peace Treaties* (1919–20) to administer former colonies of the German and *Ottoman* (Turkish) empires.

- Officially under the control of the *League of Nations*, government of the colonies was given to the Allied powers until such time as the mandates were ready for independence.

m

- Most mandated territories received independence after the Second World War.
- **TIP** The mandates were an important part of the Paris Peace Settlement. The populations of many mandates, particularly in the Middle East, had wanted independence after the First World War. The treaties, however, merely replaced one set of colonial rulers with another.

Mao Zedong: the founder and first ruler of communist China.

- A member of the Communist Party since the 1920s, he took part in the 'Long March' of 1934–35.
- He was responsible for developing the *guerrilla warfare* methods used by the communists in their civil war with the nationalists. From the creation of the communist state in 1949 up to 1961, Mao made China an ally of the *USSR*.
- Under Mao's autocratic leadership China developed its own version of communism. An attempt to modernise the economy through the *Great Leap Forward* (1958–60) proved disastrous. Millions of people died.
- In 1966 Mao initiated the *Cultural Revolution*, with the aim of removing senior party officials from office.
- In 1972 he normalised relations with the USA. Communist China was admitted to the *UN*, with a seat on the Security Council.
- In his final years he allowed policy in China to be influenced by radicals — particularly his wife (Madame Mao).
- **TIP** Mao Zedong was the most important Chinese politician of the twentieth century. Study of his career is essential to an understanding of the history of East Asia.

March Offensive, 1918: a German attempt to win the war on the Western Front, before the full impact was felt of US forces arriving in Europe.

- The push was made possible by conclusion of the war on the Eastern Front, with the Treaty of *Brest-Litovsk*.
- The German attack was stopped at the second Battle of the *Marne* in July 1918. From that date the German Army was in constant retreat until the armistice was signed in November.
- **TIP** This was the turning-point in the First World War.

March on Rome, 1922: successful attempt by the *fascists* to gain power in Italy under *Mussolini*.

- The party organised a mass march on Rome, to force the resignation of the government.
- King Victor Emanuel III, fearing a civil war, gave way to fascist pressure. Mussolini was invited to form a coalition government of fascists, conservatives and nationalists.
- **TIP** The March on Rome highlighted the weakness of successive Italian governments. Subsequent events showed that Mussolini was given power, rather than being forced into seizing it.

March on Washington, 1963: a prominent demonstration, which aimed to put pressure on the *Kennedy* administration to support African American *civil rights*.

- The march culminated in a rally of some 250,000 people at the Lincoln Memorial and was noted for Martin Luther *King*'s 'I have a dream' keynote speech.
- **▨ TIP** The march and rally highlighted King as an accomplished orator and spokesman for the African American civil rights movement.

Marne Battles, 1914, 1918: major Allied successes on the Western Front in the First World War.

- In the first Battle of the Marne Franco–British forces prevented the capture of Paris.
- In the second battle (July 1918) American, British and French forces, under the command of Ferdinand Foch, repulsed the German *March Offensive*.
- **▨ TIP** Both battles defeated German armies exhausted by weeks of offensive operations. The first resulted in 4 years of trench warfare; the second ultimately brought war on the Western Front to an end.

Marshall Aid: a programme of financial assistance given by the USA to Europe for reconstruction following the Second World War (also known as the European Recovery Programme).

- Along with the *Truman Doctrine*, Marshall Aid (named after the Secretary of State) was part of the US policy to contain the spread of communism in Europe.
- Between 1948 and 1952 America gave US$17 billion in aid. The *USSR* was offered Marshall Aid, but refused.
- **▨ TIP** The 'Marshall Plan' was a huge success in helping the rapid recovery of the west European economies after the ravages of war, and thus an important plank in the US policy against communism.

Marx, Karl: philosopher and economist, who founded modern socialism and communism.

- Marx believed that the history of mankind was a struggle between competing economic classes, in which the industrial working class, the *proletariat*, would eventually triumph over factory owners and entrepreneurs (the bourgeoisie) to create a socialist society of equality.
- With Friedrich Engels he wrote the ***Communist Manifesto***, believing that the 1848 revolutions might bring social revolution to Europe.
- His chief work was a critique of the capitalist economic system, ***Capital***, which was published in 1867.
- Marx was a German Jew, who lived most of his life in London. In the 1860s he founded the first International Workingmen's Organisation.
- **▨ TIP** Marx had a massive influence on the development of socialism and communism in the nineteenth and twentieth centuries.

Matteotti Affair, 1924: a scandal which almost caused the downfall of *Mussolini*.

- Giacomo Matteotti, a socialist MP who was highly critical of the *fascists*, was found murdered shortly after the 1924 parliamentary elections. The fascists were accused of his murder.
- Several opposition MPs withdrew from Parliament in protest, which became known as the 'Aventine Secession'.

m

- However, far from removing Mussolini from power, the fascist leader used the scandal to introduce press censorship and increase his control of Parliament.
- ■ *TIP* The scandal was important in explaining how Mussolini turned his coalition government of 1922 into a dictatorship by 1925.

Mazzini, Giuseppe: Italian nationalist and revolutionary.

- In 1833 he formed *Young Italy*, to promote the idea of an Italian national state. He was involved in revolutions in Piedmont (1831) and Rome (1849).
- Exiled in 1849, never to return, Mazzini had a great influence on other Italian nationalists, such as Giuseppe *Garibaldi*.
- ■ *TIP* Mazzini was important in keeping the idea of Italian unity alive during the years of conservative repression (1815–48).

Mehemet Ali: Pasha (ruler) of Egypt, who was involved in two major crises in the *Eastern Question* (1831–33 and 1839–41), which both attracted *Great Power* intervention.

- Between 1831 and 1833 Mehemet Ali conquered Palestine and Syria, and attacked Constantinople in an attempt to overthrow the Sultan of Turkey. He was prevented only through the military intervention of Russia. In the Treaty of *Unkiar Skelessi* Russia was given the right to send warships through the Straits (the Dardanelles and Bosphorus). Mehemet Ali was given Palestine and Syria for life.
- In 1839–41 Mehemet Ali's forces in Syria were attacked by Turkey. A new crisis led to the involvement of Britain and France. In the Treaty of London (1840) the Great Powers forced Mehemet Ali to give up Syria. In the Straits Convention (1841) the Great Powers agreed to close the Straits to all warships.
- ■ *TIP* These crises are important aspects of the Eastern Question. The second is a good example of the *Concert of Europe* in operation.

Mein Kampf: a book ('My Struggle') by Adolf *Hitler*, which contained a number of the ideas associated with his rise to power.

- The book refers to Hitler's quest for *Lebensraum* (living space), his anti-communism, his *anti-Semitism* and his dislike of the Treaty of *Versailles*.
- The text was dictated to supporters such as Rudolf *Hess*, while they were imprisoned in the Landsberg Fortress in 1924–25, following the failure of the *Beer Hall Putsch*.
- ■ *TIP* Historians are divided on its significance. Some believe it contained Hitler's plans for the future. Others see it as a generalised statement of his prejudices.

Menshevik: a member of a faction of the Russian Social Democrat Party.

- The Mensheviks split with the *Bolsheviks* at the London Congress of 1903, believing that the party should be a mass-membership socialist party, as opposed to the Bolshevik demand for it to remain a group of committed revolutionaries.
- The Mensheviks also believed that, before a socialist revolution could occur in Russia, it had to be preceded by the development of a liberal parliamentary government and the creation of an industrialised economy. In 1917 *Lenin*

believed that both revolutions could occur, one straight after the other.

- Therefore the Mensheviks supported the *Provisional Government* and opposed the Bolshevik seizure of power in the *October Revolution* of 1917. They were finally banned as a party by Lenin's government in 1922.
- **TIP** Mensheviks tended to have views similar to other European socialists. Lenin, in contrast, established a new view on how to create a socialist state.

Metternich, Clemens: a leading European conservative, Austrian Foreign Minister (1809–48) and Chancellor (1835–48).

- His diplomacy from 1809 to 1815 enabled Austria to recover from its humiliating defeat by *Napoleon* in 1809. He was a major figure in creating the Fourth *Coalition* in 1812.
- He was a leading diplomat at the Congress of Vienna (1814–15), which reorganised Europe following Napoleon's defeat. Along with the Russian Tsar, Metternich was a keen opponent of liberalism. He supported the *Troppau* Protocol of 1820.
- Within the *German Confederation*, he helped suppress liberalism through the *Carlsbad Decrees* (1819). He was forced to resign in 1848, following liberal demonstrations in Vienna calling for political reform.
- His fall helped to start other liberal revolutions across the German Confederation.
- **TIP** Metternich was a leading European statesman. The suppression of liberalism by the *Holy Alliance* and the Carlsbad Decrees were known as the 'Metternich System'.

Midway, Battle of, 1942: a battle dominated by aircraft carriers, which turned out to be the turning-point in the Pacific War between the USA and Japan.

- The Japanese lost three of their four aircraft carriers, the USA one. The US Navy prevented the capture of Midway Island.
- Following the battle, the USA went on the offensive, launching an island-hopping campaign against Japanese possessions in the Pacific, until they were within aerial bombing distance of Japan.
- **TIP** The battle highlighted the critical importance of naval air power in the Pacific War.

Miliukov, Paul: leader of the *Kadet* Party in Russia.

- He returned to Russia from exile following the *Revolution of 1905* and was a member of the third and fourth *Dumas* before the First World War.
- He was a leading figure in the creation of the progressive bloc during the war, demanding political reform.
- Following the *February Revolution* he was made Foreign Minister. However, his popularity declined because of his support for continuing the war on the Eastern Front.
- **TIP** Miliukov's later career highlighted the dilemma of liberal politicians in Russia. He wanted to support the Western Allies against Germany, but was faced with the need to save Russia from the costs and pressures of fighting a major war.

Mirabeau, Count: a leading moderate during the early stages of the French Revolution.

- He was in favour of constitutional monarchy and attempted to persuade *Louis XVI* to accept political change.
- He was a member of the Committee of Thirty, represented the Third Estate in the *Estates General*, and took part in the Constituent Assembly.
- His early death (1791) deprived the moderates of an effective leader.

TIP Mirabeau represented the moderate reformers who were swept away with the creation of the *First Republic* in 1792.

***Mittelstand*:** the 'lower middle class' in interwar Germany, who were important supporters of the Nazi Party (1930–33).

- Comprising shopkeepers, clerks, small farmers and white collar workers, this social group suffered badly in the hyperinflation of 1922–24, when they lost their savings. They also saw threats to their livelihood from the growth of powerful trade unions and big business.
- When *Hitler* became Chancellor he passed laws specifically to aid the *Mittelstand*, such as the Entailed Farm Act of 1933 and a ban on the development of department stores.

TIP Hitler's need to woo big business to support his rearmament programme led him to abandon many of the economic demands of this social group.

Molotov, Vyacheslav: Soviet Foreign Minister (1939–49), who negotiated the *Nazi–Soviet Pact* (1939) whereby Germany and the *USSR* partitioned Poland and eastern Europe between them.

- During the Second World War he accompanied *Stalin* to all the major Allied conferences.
- His poor relationship with President *Truman* was an important reason for the deterioration in US–Soviet relations after 1945.

Montgomery Bus Boycott, 1955–56: a victory for the African American *civil rights* movement, which brought Martin Luther *King* to national prominence.

- Using King's policy of non-violent protest, African Americans in Montgomery successfully desegregated the city's buses after a year-long boycott.
- Martin Luther King maintained African American solidarity, despite intimidation by Whites.
- The boycott was helped by the *Supreme Court* decision of 1956, which declared segregated buses unconstitutional and led to the creation of the Southern Christian Leadership Conference to campaign for desegregation.

TIP The boycott was the first major victory for non-violent protest, which became a feature of King's campaign for civil rights.

Moroccan Crisis, 1905–06: an international crisis caused by German opposition to French colonial interests in Morocco. Germany attempted to use the crisis to split the newly formed *Entente Cordiale* between Britain and France.

- Although Germany achieved the dismissal of the French Foreign Minister, the plan backfired. At the Algeciras Conference on Morocco (1906) Germany was supported only by Austria-Hungary. Britain supported France. The conference agreed that Morocco could be partitioned between France and Spain.

■ *TIP* This was a critical event in European relations. It increased cooperation between Britain and France, as well as British suspicions of German policy. As a result, the crisis can be seen as a distant cause of the First World War.

Münchengratz Agreement, 1833: a renewal of the *Holy Alliance* (1815) by Austria, Russia and Prussia.

● The meeting took place following their suppression of the Polish Revolt of 1830–31. The three *Great Powers* restated their support for conservative, autocratic monarchy and their opposition to liberal ideas, such as parliamentary government.

■ *TIP* The agreement split the Great Powers into conservative and liberal camps in the 1830s and 1840s.

Munich Crisis, 1938: a major European crisis over the German demand for annexation of German-speaking areas of Czechoslovakia, known as the *Sudetenland.*

● The crisis was resolved by the Munich Agreement between Germany, Britain, France and Italy.

● Czechoslovakia was forced to cede the Sudetenland to Germany. The agreement led to the partition of Czechoslovakia, with both Poland and Hungary acquiring territory.

● The crisis and subsequent agreement offer the best example of the *appeasement* policies followed by Britain and France towards Germany.

■ *TIP* The crisis delayed a European war by a year. In March 1939 Germany occupied the Czech-speaking areas of Bohemia and Moravia. Britain and France abandoned appeasement and signed an agreement to defend Poland.

Mussolini, Benito: the founder of Italian *fascism* and Prime Minister of Italy (1922–43).

● Originally a socialist, Mussolini formed the Fascist Party in 1919. It was anti-socialist, anti-democratic and strongly nationalist.

● Mussolini established a fascist dictatorship in 1925 and set about creating a colonial empire. His only achievement in this sphere was the conquest of *Abyssinia* (1935–36).

● In 1936 Mussolini became an ally of *Hitler* and in 1940 joined Germany in the Second World War.

● Mussolini's participation in the war proved disastrous for Italy. Abyssinia was lost in 1941 and Libya in 1942. In 1943 British and US forces invaded Italy. Mussolini was forced to resign.

● He was murdered in 1945 by Italian communist partisans.

■ *TIP* Mussolini is an example of a right-wing politician in the interwar period who opposed parliamentary democracy in favour of strong, nationalist rule.

Napoleon: a member of the *Consulate* (1799–1804) and Emperor of France (1804–14), an outstanding general and statesman, whose military victories led to the domination of Europe by France. (Also referred to as Napoleon I).

- He rose to prominence as a result of his military campaign in Italy in 1796–97 and took power in the *Coup of 18th Brumaire* (1799).
- By 1810 Napoleon had defeated Austria, Prussia and Russia and conquered Spain, Italy and central Europe. Only Britain remained undefeated.
- After 1810 the Napoleonic empire began to decline. The *Continental blockade* against Britain did not succeed. His attack on Russia in 1812 ended in disaster, with the destruction of the **Grande Armée**. He was finally defeated by the Fourth *Coalition* and abdicated in 1814.
- Forced into exile on Elba, Napoleon then returned to power for '100 Days' in 1815, which ended with his defeat at *Waterloo*. He was exiled and imprisoned on the island of St Helena, where he died in 1821.
- Domestically, Napoleon introduced legal reform to France (the *Napoleonic Code*) and made a *concordat* with the Pope.

■ *TIP* Napoleon was the dominant European statesman at the beginning of the nineteenth century. Historians are divided on whether he destroyed or saved the main principles of the French Revolution.

Napoleon III: President of the *Second Republic* (1848–52) and Emperor of France (1852–70).

- A nephew of Napoleon I, he used the Napoleonic legend to be elected President in 1848.
- Under the Republican constitution he was allowed only one 4-year term as President so, in 1851, he overthrew the constitution and made himself President for life. A year later he declared himself Emperor. In both cases his move was endorsed by a referendum.
- Napoleon III attempted to recreate France as Europe's major power. With Britain, he fought and defeated Russia in the *Crimean War* (1854–56) and defeated Austria in Italy (1859).
- He failed in his attempt to create an empire in Mexico (1864–67) and also failed to intervene in the war between Prussia and Austria (1866).

- He began to rule his empire as a dictator, but after 1860 allowed more political freedom. In 1869 he became a constitutional monarch.
- He fought the *Franco–Prussian War* (1870–71) without allies; his defeat led to the fall of the empire and the creation of the Third Republic.
- **TIP** Napoleon III was an important figure in international relations between 1848 and 1870, and influenced the unification of both Italy and Germany. His attempt to recreate a Napoleonic empire failed on the battlefield, not from opposition within France.

Napoleonic Code: reform of the Civil Law by *Napoleon*, which became law in 1804.

- Rights of individual property were confirmed, as was the dominance of a husband in marriage, with women given inferior legal status. Divorce was made more difficult.
- The code owed more to the laws of the *ancien régime* than the Revolution. Its tough views were mirrored in the new Criminal Code and Penal Law. Hard labour and branding for crimes were restored, trial by jury was severely limited, *lettres de cachet*, which allowed arrest without trial (and which had been in use before 1789), was restored in 1810.
- Later the code was extended to parts of French-occupied Europe.
- **TIP** The code raises the question: did Napoleon save or destroy the French Revolution?

National Industrial Recovery Act, 1933: an important component of the first *New Deal*, which set up the National Recovery Administration (NRA) to control prices, set wages and monitor union recognition.

- This was an attempt by President *Roosevelt* to boost the US economy out of depression.
- The NRA codes were disliked by many businesses. Ford refused to participate.
- The NRA was declared unconstitutional by the US *Supreme Court* in the Schecter *Sick Chicken Case* of 1935, because the federal government had exceeded its powers.
- **TIP** The NRA was central to the first New Deal. It shows how Roosevelt wished to increase the use of federal government in economic affairs.

National Liberal Party: a German political party (1866–1918), which received electoral support from business and the industrial class.

- The party was a staunch supporter of *Bismarck*'s policy for the unification of Germany between 1866 and 1878. Bismarck split with the party by abandoning free trade and introducing protective tariffs in 1878–79.
- After 1918 it formed the basis for the German People's Party.
- **TIP** More 'nationalist' than 'liberal', the party supported free trade, big business and a free press.

National Recovery Administration (NRA): see *National Industrial Recovery Act*.

National Security Council: coordinates policy for internal and external security in the USA.

n

- It was established under the National Security Act (1947) and became part of the *Executive Office of the Presidency*.
- Permanent members are the President, the Vice-President, the Secretaries of State and Defense, the Director of the *CIA* and the Chair of the Joint Chiefs of Staff.
- *Kennedy* introduced the post of National Security Adviser to the President in 1962. The Council was the main decision-making body during the *Cuban Missile Crisis* (1962).
- Under *Nixon*, Henry *Kissinger* was the National Security Adviser and he played a major role in negotiating *détente* and forging links with communist China.
- **TIP** The National Security Council was one of the most important decision-making bodies in US foreign policy during the *Cold War*.

national self-determination: reflected a belief that the internal stability of states would be best assured if they were based on one racial or language group.

- The concept was closely associated with President *Wilson* and the *Paris Peace Treaties* (1919–20).
- The new states of Latvia, Lithuania and Estonia were based on this concept, as was the revival of Poland as an independent state. It was used to remove Posen and Alsace-Lorraine from Germany.
- However, the principle was not always followed in the treaties: Austria was forbidden to join with Germany, and Czechoslovakia was created containing Czechs, Slovaks, Germans, Hungarians and Ukrainians.
- More recently, the disintegration of the *USSR* and Yugoslavia were based mainly on national self-determination.
- **TIP** Application of the principle helped to destroy the Austro-Hungarian and *Ottoman* (Turkish) empires after the First World War. It also led to war and instability in southeast Europe in the 1990s.

National Workshops: a form of unemployment relief created in France following the *February Revolution of 1848*.

- The Republican National Assembly declared the right to work for all men and guaranteed manual work for the unemployed in the Workshops.
- The abolition of National Workshops led to the *June Days* insurrection in Paris. Over 3,000 were killed when General Cavaignac restored order.
- **TIP** The National Workshops showed the socialist side of the *Second Republic*. Their abolition showed how the National Assembly had moved to the right. Following the June Days, the Second Republic was dominated by the middle class.

NATO: see *North Atlantic Treaty Organisation*.

Nazi–Soviet Pact, 1939: an agreement laying the ground for Germany and the *USSR* to attack and partition Poland. It was also agreed that the USSR could reoccupy the Baltic States.

- Known also as the Molotov–Ribbentrop Pact or the Hitler–Stalin Pact, it prevented the possibility of *Hitler* having to fight a war on two fronts (against

Britain and France in the West and the USSR in the East) when he invaded Poland.

- *Stalin* supposedly signed the pact in order to gain time to rebuild the *Red Army* after the *Purges*, and to provide a barrier against future German invasion.
- The pact permitted the rapid defeat of Poland in 1939, and the Soviet occupation of Latvia, Lithuania and Estonia in 1940.
- **TIP** The pact made war with Poland inevitable. It ended any possible co-operation between Britain and France with the USSR.

neo-guelfism: an idea, put forward by the Italian nationalist Gioberti, for the unification of Italy.

- In 1847 he proposed a federation of Italian states, with the Pope as President. This would have allowed existing monarchs to remain on their thrones.
- The idea gained credibility with the election of Pope Pius IX in 1846. The Pope's Christian humanity was misinterpreted as liberalism by Gioberti and his supporters.
- Following the 1848–49 Revolution, in which the Pope was forced to leave Rome by liberal revolutionaries, Pius IX became a staunch opponent of Italian nationalism and liberalism.
- **TIP** This was an example of the many proposals for the creation of an Italian state. Eventually Italy was unified by the expansion of Piedmont-Sardinia.

NEP: see *New Economic Policy*.

New Deal: a programme of social and economic reform undertaken by the administration of Franklin D. *Roosevelt* (1933–41).

- It aimed to bring relief to the poor and the unemployed, sought recovery from economic depression, and introduced reform to the economic system to prevent future depressions.
- The programme unfolded under the first New Deal (1933–35), the second New Deal (1935–37) and the third New Deal (1937–39).
- It was characterised by the creation of federal agencies and administrations, with specific (and at times conflicting) tasks.
- The popularity of the New Deal led to Roosevelt's re-election in 1936 and 1940. It brought partial economic recovery. Full recovery came only with the outbreak of the Second World War.
- **TIP** The New Deal helped to save the USA from the worst aspects of the Depression and brought major social changes. It greatly increased the power of the federal government, but was criticised for lack of long-term planning.

New Economic Policy (NEP), 1921–28: a major policy change made by *Lenin*, replacing *war communism*.

- Lenin recognised the failures of war communism, which had led to a fall in production and to famine in the countryside. The NEP permitted the private ownership of farms and small businesses. The most important industries, however, remained under state control.

- It brought about economic recovery, but left unresolved the problem of peasant ownership of land in a communist state.
- It was ended by *Stalin*, when he ordered the forced *collectivisation* of agriculture and rapid industrialisation.

TIP The NEP showed Lenin to be a pragmatic politician. He realised the shortcomings of war communism. However, he left it to Stalin to bring about a further social and economic revolution.

New Frontier: President *Kennedy*'s programme for social justice at home and resistance to communism overseas.

- Kennedy's domestic programme faced major problems because of the conservative coalition in *Congress* between Republicans and Southern Democrats.
- He was forced to respond on *civil rights* by activists in the *freedom rides* and in southern universities.
- Overseas, Kennedy faced failure in the *Bay of Pigs* fiasco and the *Berlin Wall Crisis* (both 1961). He attempted to resist communism in Southeast Asia through support for South Vietnam and a *CIA*-sponsored war against communists in Laos. His major success was the removal of Soviet missiles from *Cuba* (1962).

TIP The New Frontier programme should be seen as a continuation of *Truman*'s Fair Deal policies plus *containment*.

new imperialism: a term applied to the period of rapid colonial expansion by the major European powers, 1870–1914.

- By the time of the First World War, virtually all of Africa was under European control.
- This rapid imperialist expansion was due to a variety of factors, such as the search for new markets, the lack of opportunities for expansion in Europe, and a belief in European racial superiority (*Social Darwinism*).
- Germany's attempt to 'catch up' in colonial expansion, the *Weltpolitik* (1897–1914), helped to create conditions for the outbreak of the First World War.

TIP The most noted aspect of new imperialism was the partition of Africa (or *Scramble for Africa*), 1880–1914.

New Look foreign policy: a policy stance adopted by the *Eisenhower* administration from 1953 onwards, differing from *containment* in its attempt to roll back communism around the world.

- In reality the New Look differed only slightly from containment in its attitude to communist states.
- The main difference was in the nature of US defence. Eisenhower placed great emphasis on the development of nuclear, rather than conventional, forces. This change was associated with brinkmanship and the threat of nuclear attack as a diplomatic tactic, used by the Secretary of State, John Foster *Dulles*.

TIP In questions on US foreign policy after 1945 you need to identify the similarities and differences between *Truman*'s and Eisenhower's policies towards communism.

Nicholas I: Russian Tsar, 1825–55.

- Known as the 'Policeman of Europe' because of his defence of conservatism and opposition to liberal revolution, he continued support for *Alexander I's* *Holy Alliance* in the *Münchengratz Agreement* (1833) with Austria and Prussia. He assisted Austria in defeating the Hungarian Revolution in 1849.
- However, he also followed the traditional Russian policy of expansion at the expense of the *Ottoman* (Turkish) *empire*. Russia fought against Turkey in 1828–29 and again in the *Crimean War* (1853–56). At home, Nicholas maintained strict control of government, opposing all demands for reform. At his death, Russia was on the brink of defeat at the hands of Britain, France and Turkey.
- *TIP* Nicholas I was closely linked with the maintenance of absolute monarchy. However, his policies towards Turkey threatened the European *balance of power* and caused the first *Great Power* war since 1815.

Nicholas II: Russian Tsar, 1894–1917 (the last tsar).

- Like his predecessor, *Alexander III*, he supported the idea of an autocratic monarchy. However, he lacked his father's ability and strength of character. He was much influenced by his German wife, the Tsarina Alexandra.
- He was faced with serious social and political unrest, which resulted in the *Revolution of 1905*. Forced to make political concessions, he agreed to the creation of a national parliament (the *Duma*) and some limited reforms.
- In foreign affairs, Russia became a close military ally of France. Attempts to expand Russian influence in the Far East led to defeat in the *Russo–Japanese War* (1904–05). The decision to enter the First World War also proved disastrous.
- Military defeat and the economic strains of war led to the *February Revolution of 1917*. Nicholas II's decision to abdicate on behalf of himself and his young son, Alexis, brought tsarist rule to an end.
- *TIP* Nicholas II's character was an important factor in creating the conditions for revolution in both 1905 and 1917.

Night of the Long Knives, 1934: the murder of *Hitler's* political opponents by the *SS*.

- The main casualties were the leadership of the *SA* (stormtroopers). Under Ernst Roehm, the SA wanted radical social policies and demanded to be a major military force.
- Hitler feared Roehm as a potential rival and also wanted Army support for his foreign policy programme.
- *TIP* This event consolidated Hitler's control on power. He had removed his chief rivals in the Nazi Party. When President *Hindenburg* died in August 1934 the Army supported Hitler's decision to become President as well as Chancellor.

nihilism: a radical political movement in Russia during the reign of *Alexander II* (1855–81), associated with the terror organisation 'The People's Will'.

- Nihilists believed that improvement in the social and political condition of Russia could occur only through the elimination of the Tsar and his advisers. The group was responsible for the murder of tsarist officials in the 1870s.
- Its most notorious act was the assassination of Alexander II in 1881.

Nivelle Offensive, 1917: a failed offensive, which led to the French Army mutiny.

- As Commander-in-Chief on the Western Front, Nivelle launched mass attacks against German defences, which resulted in over 100,000 casualties.
- Following on from the slaughter in the Battle of *Verdun* in 1916, many French units mutinied. Order was restored only with the replacement of Nivelle by Marshal Pétain, the hero of Verdun.

■ *TIP* The offensive and the subsequent mutiny reflected increasing war weariness and opposition to the tactics of mass infantry attacks.

Nixon, Richard: US President (1969–74), whose foreign policy successes included *détente* (1971) and the *SALT* I Treaty (1972) on nuclear arms with the *USSR*, and the normalisation of relations with communist China (1972).

- Much controversy surrounds Nixon's handling of the *Vietnam War*. The invasion of Cambodia in 1970, and the massive bombing of North Vietnam, were heavily criticised at home and abroad. Nevertheless, in 1973 Nixon signed a peace agreement with North Vietnam, which saw the withdrawal of US troops from Southeast Asia.
- At home, he faced the *Watergate Scandal*, involving illegal activities during the 1972 presidential election. To avoid impeachment (dismissal), Nixon resigned in 1974.

■ *TIP* Although a highly controversial politician, Nixon proved to be a very effective statesman, especially in foreign affairs.

NKVD (People's Commissariat for Internal Affairs)**:** Russian secret police, created in 1934 as a successor to the *OGPU*.

- It administered the *Gulag* concentration camp system.
- Its main task was to organise the *Purges* (1934–39). Under the leadership of Yagoda, Yezhov and *Beria*, the NKVD arrested hundreds of thousands of Soviet citizens. Tens of thousands were executed without trial, others used as slave labour.

■ *TIP* The actions of the NKVD revealed the totalitarian nature of *Stalin*'s dictatorship. The random arrest of Soviet citizens created a climate of fear and terror.

North Atlantic Treaty Organisation (NATO), 1949: a defence organisation created after the *Berlin Airlift Crisis* and a major bulwark of US policy for the *containment* of communism.

- Its chief role was in defence of the West during the *Cold War*. Dominated by the USA, in 1949 it included Britain, Italy, the Low Countries, France, Norway, Denmark, Iceland and Portugal. Expanded to include Greece and Turkey, the admission of West Germany in 1955 caused East–West tension. France officially withdrew in 1966.
- Major strains appeared in the organisation in the early 1980s, with the US deployment of Cruise and Pershing II missiles in Europe.
- Since the end of the Cold War (1991), some Eastern Bloc states, such as Poland and Hungary, have joined NATO as a defence against Russian dominance. The

first use of NATO forces in a non-Cold War context occurred in Kosovo (1999), which had been invaded by Serbia.

■ *TIP* NATO was a key organisation in Europe during the Cold War. Its Eastern equivalent was the *Warsaw Pact*.

North German Confederation, 1867–71: created by *Bismarck,* following the Prussian victory in the *Seven Weeks' War* (1866), replacing the *German Confederation*.

● It contained the German states north of the River Main and was dominated by Prussia. The south German states of Baden, Bavaria and Württemberg were outside the Confederation, but were in military alliance with Prussia.

● Its constitution formed the basis of the German imperial constitution of 1871–1918.

■ *TIP* The new Confederation was a clear example of Bismarck's diplomatic skill, ensuring Prussia's dominant position in Germany.

NSC–68, 1950: a report by the *National Security Council* proposing major rearmament by the USA.

● The report was drawn up by Paul Nitze, following the *USSR*'s successful testing of a nuclear bomb.

● With the outbreak of the *Korean War* (1950), the US government accepted its recommendations.

● The massive US arms build-up in the 1950s led to the creation of the so-called military–industrial complex, an interdependence between US industry and the military.

■ *TIP* The report influenced the decision to escalate the arms race with the USSR.

Nuremberg Laws, 1935: German *anti-Semitic* laws introduced by the Nazis, which took away citizenship from German Jews and forbade marriage between Jews and Germans.

● This was one of the first attempts by the Nazis to persecute and humiliate the Jews. Following the announcement, many German Jews attempted to flee the country.

■ *TIP* The laws revealed the reality of Nazi policy towards the Jews and emphasised the Nazi notion of racial purity.

October Manifesto of 1905: a promise of reform made by Tsar *Nicholas II*, at the height of the *Revolution of 1905*.

- On the advice of *Witte*, Nicholas II declared his intention to introduce civil liberties and establish an elected national parliament, the *Duma*.
- The manifesto had the effect of splitting the opposition to the Tsar's government. Moderates accepted Nicholas's declaration. Radicals continued to demand change, organising strikes and demonstrations.
- This gave the Tsar the opportunity to regain control, but when the *Fundamental Law of 1906* was published Nicholas back-tracked on many of his promises. He retained the right to appoint and dismiss ministers and to issue decrees when the Duma was not in session.
- **TIP** The manifesto explains how the Tsar was able to survive the 1905 Revolution. The alternative would have been to create a military dictatorship, which could have resulted in civil war.

October Revolution of 1917: the *Bolshevik* seizure of power in Russia which, unlike the *February Revolution*, was carefully planned by the Military Revolutionary Committee under the guidance of Leon *Trotsky*.

- Centring mainly on Petrograd, it began with the capture by Red Guards of the *Provisional Government* in the Winter Palace. Its timing coincided with a Bolshevik majority in the All-Russia Soviet of Workers', Peasants' and Soldiers' Deputies.
- *Lenin* used this majority to gain approval for the Bolshevik take-over.
- **TIP** Controversy still surrounds the October Revolution. Was it the act of a small, unrepresentative group, or did it have popular support?

Octobrist: a member of the Russian liberal group the Union of 17th October, founded by Dimitri Shipov, leader of the *zemstvo* movement.

- Members accepted the *October Manifesto* as the political structure for Russia and were willing to work with the Tsar's government to make it a success.
- They gained 17 seats in the first *Duma*, but increased these to 120 in the third (1907).
- **TIP** Russian liberalism after 1905 split between the Octobrists and the more radical *Kadets*.

OGPU (United State Political Administration)**:** the Soviet secret police, which replaced the GPU (State Political Administration) in 1923, when it became an independent institution.

- It was used by *Stalin* to enforce collectivisation (1928–34) and to organise and administer the first Show Trials.
- It was replaced by the *NKVD* in 1934.

Okhrana: tsarist secret police, which used the system of internal passports to maintain surveillance of the Russian population.

- It also organised camps in Siberia for prisoners in internal exile.

OKW (*Oberkommando der Wehrmacht*)**:** headquarters of the German armed forces during the Second World War.

Olmütz, 1850: an agreement to re-establish the *German Confederation* after the 1848–49 revolutions.

- It was regarded as a triumph for the Austrian Chancellor, Schwarzenburg, who regained Austrian chairmanship of the Confederation.
- However, it was viewed as a setback by many Prussians. Prussia was forced to dissolve the Erfurt Union of German states, created in 1849 under Prussian leadership.

TIP The agreement emphasised Austrian leadership in German affairs.

Order No. 1 of Petrograd Soviet, 1917: declared that all military orders had to be subject to the consent of elected soldiers' councils, which had the effect of undermining military discipline.

- This was used by *Bolshevik* agitators to spread support for ending the war with Germany.

TIP The order reflected political instability in Russia after the *February Revolution*. Power was shared between the *Provisional Government* and the *Soviet*. This situation was exploited effectively by *Lenin*.

Ordinances of St Cloud, 1830: decrees by *Charles X*, which dissolved the parliament before it had a chance to meet, increased press censorship and increased the property qualification for voting.

- The decrees were made following the poor showing of government supporters in parliamentary elections.
- They led directly to the 'Three Glorious Days' of rioting in Paris, which brought down the government of Polignac and the Bourbon monarchy.

TIP This was the immediate cause of the *July Revolution*.

Ostpolitik: agreements for an 'Eastern policy' between East and West Germany (1970–72), accepting that Germany was divided into two states, and also recognising the East German–Polish border.

- They were mainly the work of the Social Democrat Chancellor of West Germany, Willy *Brandt*. Largely as a result of *Ostpolitik*, Brandt won the Nobel peace price in 1971.
- The agreements led to both East and West Germany joining the *United Nations* in 1974.

■ *TIP* The agreements should be seen in the broader context of *détente* between East and West.

Ottoman empire: a large east European and Asiatic empire, ruled by Muslim sultans from Constantinople (Istanbul), which reached the height of its power in the seventeenth century.

● From the 1680s onwards it declined in power and influence, losing territory to both Austria and Russia.

● In the nineteenth century its decline affected international relations, giving rise to the *Eastern Question*. It fought wars with Russia in 1828–29, 1853–56 and 1877–78.

● By the late nineteenth century Ottoman control of the *Balkans* was undermined by the growth of nationalism. In 1912–13 the Balkan League defeated what was now known as Turkey, and took control of virtually all Turkish territory in Europe. Turkey fought on the side of Germany and Austria-Hungary in the First World War.

● The empire collapsed in 1920, to be replaced by the Turkish Republic.

■ *TIP* The long decline of the Ottoman empire was a major issue in nineteenth- and early twentieth-century international relations.

OVRA: Italian secret police during *Mussolini*'s rule.

Pact of Steel, 1939: an agreement between Germany and Italy, committing them to support each other in the event of war.

- The pact was not honoured by Italy when Germany went to war in September 1939. Italy entered the war in June 1940.
- It upset British and French hopes that *Mussolini* could be separated from Germany.
- Together with the *Nazi–Soviet Pact* (1939), it ensured that *Hitler* would not have to fight a war on two fronts when he invaded Poland.

■ *TIP* The pact was signed 1 month after Mussolini had annexed Albania. With the Aix Agreement (1936) and the *Anti-Comintern Pact* (1937), the Pact of Steel showed how close Germany and Italy had become diplomatically.

Palmerston, Lord: Foreign Secretary (1830–34, 1835–41, 1846–51) and Prime Minister (1855–58, 1859–65), who dominated British foreign policy for over 30 years. He followed the principle that Britain had no permanent friends or enemies when it came to defending British interests. He encouraged trade and avoided major conflicts with the *Great Powers*, with the exception of the *Crimean War*.

- His habit of making decisions without consultation resulted in his dismissal in 1851, after he recognised Louis Napoleon's (*Napoleon III*) coup in France.
- He followed policies similar to those of his predecessor, *Canning*, such as opposing the slave trade.

■ *TIP* Palmerston was the most towering figure in British politics between the fall of Peel (1846) and his death in 1865.

Panama Scandal, 1892: a major financial scandal in the Third Republic, which highlighted French *anti-Semitism*.

- Financial failure of the Panama Canal Company revealed that some of its directors had bribed ministers and deputies of the National Assembly in 1888.
- Two of the main culprits were Jews, and the discovery was used by anti-Semites to attack Jews in general. Edouard Dumont, who had founded the National Anti-Semitic League, launched an attack on the government.
- Several leading politicians had their careers ruined, including the former Prime Minister Freycinet.

p

■ *TIP* The scandal brought to an end the 'opportunist' period of dominance in the Third Republic.

Pan-German League, 1890–1939: an extreme German nationalist organisation (the *Alldeutscher Verband*, ADV), which wanted to unite all German-speaking peoples.

- It wanted Germany to follow an aggressive foreign and colonial policy.
- It also encouraged the idea of German colonisation of eastern Europe, which was a forerunner of *Hitler*'s *Lebensraum* (living space) policy.

■ *TIP* This was an important interest group in the Germany of *William I* and *William II*, which pressed the government to adopt *Weltpolitik*.

pan-Slavism: a movement that promoted greater cooperation between the Slavonic-speaking peoples.

- It gained popularity in Russia, which regarded itself as the guardian of Slav interests.
- It reached the height of its influence in the *Great Eastern Crisis* (1875–78), when Russia went to war with Turkey to protect the Slav people of the *Balkans*, such as the Serbs and Bulgars. The Treaty of *San Stefano* (1878) was regarded as a pan-Slav peace, because it created a large Bulgarian state.
- The idea was also important in the decade before the First World War, when Russia was an ally of Serbia.

■ *TIP* Pan-Slavism was an important concept in the *Eastern Question*, and in Russian foreign policy in the nineteenth and early twentieth centuries.

papal infallibility: a belief that the Pope cannot be in error when making statements on religion.

- It was proclaimed at the First Vatican Council of the Catholic Church in 1869–70, at the time when the Pope lost his last territorial possession, the patrimony of St Peter (the area around Rome).
- This caused concern in European states that the Pope was trying to increase his authority over Catholics. In the period 1870–1914 the German, French and Italian governments all came into conflict with the Catholic Church over issues such as education.

■ *TIP* This is an important term in understanding Church–state relations in the late nineteenth century.

Papal States: territory in Italy ruled by the Pope.

- In the early nineteenth century it contained the provinces of Umbria, Romagna and the Patrimony of St Peter.
- The existence of the Papal States posed problems for Italian nationalists. Any attempt to incorporate the Papal States into a united Italy would alienate Catholics, who formed the bulk of the Italian people. Gioberti's proposal for *neo-guelfism* was a potential solution to this dilemma.
- When Italy was finally unified (1870) the Pope encouraged Catholics not to participate in politics. In 1929 the *Lateran Treaties* recreated a Papal State in the form of the Vatican City.

■ *TIP* The Papal States were a stumbling block in the unification of Italy.

Paris, Treaty of, 1856: ended the *Crimean War*.

- Russia ceded southern Bessarabia to Turkey and agreed not to build a fleet in the Black Sea.
- The former Turkish provinces of Moldavia and Wallachia were given independence, but were not allowed to join together.
- International piracy was outlawed and the *Ottoman* (Turkish) *empire* was admitted to the *Concert of Europe*.
- The treaty met all of Britain's war aims. Although France had provided the bulk of the military forces, it received nothing in return except the prestige of holding the treaty negotiations in Paris.

■ *TIP* This was another development in the evolution of the *Eastern Question*, but the terms of the treaty did not last long. Moldavia and Wallachia united in 1858, becoming the Kingdom of Romania in 1861. Russia revoked the Black Sea clauses of the treaty in 1870.

Paris Peace Treaties, 1919–20: formally brought to an end the First World War.

- The major treaty was between the Allies and Germany — the Treaty of *Versailles*, signed in 1919.
- The others were the Treaty of St Germain, with Austria (1920), the Treaty of Neuilly, with Bulgaria (1919), the Treaty of Trainon, with Hungary (1919) andthe Treaty of *Sèvres*, with the *Ottoman empire* (1920). The final treaty never came into force, due to the creation of the Turkish Republic and the Graeco–Turkish War (1920–23). It was replaced by the Treaty of Lausanne (1923).

■ *TIP* The Paris Treaties confirmed the end of the German, Austro-Hungarian and Russian empires. They created considerable bitterness in Germany, Italy and Hungary, and can be regarded as a substantial cause of international instability leading to war in 1939.

Paris Peace Treaties, 1947: agreements between the Allies (Britain, France, the USA and the *USSR*) and Germany's allies (Italy, Hungary, Finland, Bulgaria and Romania) following the Second World War.

- Italy lost the port of *Fiume* and Istria to Yugoslavia, and also lost the Dodecanese to Greece.
- Trieste became a free city.
- Romania regained Transylvania, which had been given to Hungary in 1941. It lost Moldavia to the USSR.
- Hungary was returned to its 1938 borders.
- Finland lost Karelia to the USSR and had to lease naval bases to the Soviet Navy.

■ *TIP* The Allies did not sign a peace treaty with either Germany or Austria. The Austrian State Treaty was signed in 1955, on withdrawal of the Allied armies. A peace agreement involving Germany was not entered into until the 1970s.

Pearl Harbor, 1941: a surprise Japanese air attack on the US naval base in Hawaii, which resulted in the USA entering the Second World War.

p

- The Japanese action followed a US embargo on oil to Japan (1940), when Japanese forces occupied French Indo-China.
- The Japanese attack was an attempt to force America to lift the embargo and allow Japan a free hand in East Asia. The intention was to sink the US aircraft carrier force, but on the day of the attack the aircraft carriers were at sea.
- **TIP** The attack led to war between the USA and Japan, not Germany. A German declaration of war on the USA a few days later meant that America also became involved in the European theatre.

Peninsular War, 1808–14: fought by a British-led force under the Duke of Wellington, expelling the French from Portugal and Spain.

- The campaign was regarded as the 'Spanish ulcer' by *Napoleon*, because it took troops away from his other campaigns. It thus undermined French rule in Europe and was Britain's major contribution to Napoleon's defeat.
- **TIP** Watch the spelling. It was called the Peninsula**r** War because it was fought in the Iberian peninsula.

perestroika: a Russian term meaning 'restructuring', referring to a policy introduced in the *USSR* by *Gorbachev* in 1985.

- In an attempt to end stagnation in the Soviet economy by reducing central planning, the policy introduced self-management into factories. It had a limited impact on economic performance and failed to prevent the collapse of the USSR in 1991.
- **TIP** *Perestroika* was associated with its twin policy of *glasnost* (openness), which together formed the basis of Gorbachev's reforms (1985–91).

permanent world revolution: the idea that communism could succeed only through actively spreading its influence abroad by the use of force.

- It was associated with *Trotsky* and his supporters in the 1920s, but was opposed by *Stalin*, who advocated *socialism in one country*. Stalin and his followers believed that communism could succeed only if it was firmly established in the *USSR* first.
- **TIP** Trotsky's support for the concept was one of the reasons why he failed to succeed *Lenin* as Soviet leader in 1924.

Petrograd: the name for the city of St Petersburg from 1914 to 1924.

- The name was changed from German to Russian, due to patriotic feeling at the outbreak of the First World War.
- In 1924 the name was changed to Leningrad, in honour of the *Bolshevik* leader. It reverted to St Petersburg following the collapse of communism in the 1990s.

Phoenix Programme: an attempt to capture or assassinate communist sympathisers in South Vietnam during the *Vietnam War*.

- Organised by the *Central Intelligence Agency* (CIA), its aim was to infiltrate pro-communist organisations to uncover and destroy support for the *Vietcong*. It became associated with indiscriminate political assassinations. District officers in charge of the programme were given 'headcount' targets.

- The controversial programme was heavily criticised in the USA and helped to undermine support for the war.

■ *TIP* This desperate US initiative was designed to counter the *guerrilla warfare* tactics of the Vietcong.

Plain, the: the name given to moderate members of the French Revolutionary *Convention*, who supported the overthrow of *Robespierre* in the *Themidorian Reaction*.

plebiscite: a vote on a single issue; an alternative name for a referendum.

- Plebiscites were held successfully by *Napoleon III* between 1851 and 1870, to demonstrate popular support for his actions.
- They were also used as part of the Treaty of *Versailles*. Plebiscites were held in Schleswig, Upper Silesia and East Prussia, to determine to which state each area wished to belong.

■ *TIP* The term plebiscite has tended to be replaced by referendum since the Second World War.

Plombières, Secret Pact of, 1858: an agreement between *Napoleon III* and Piedmont-Sardinia that, if a war broke out within 6 months between Austria and Piedmont-Sardinia, France would support Piedmont-Sardinia with an army of 200,000 troops.

- It was also agreed that Princess Clothilde of Piedmont-Sardinia would marry Napoleon's son, Jerome.
- The pact gave *Cavour*, the Piedmontese Prime Minister, the military support he needed to acquire the Austrian provinces of Lombardy and Venetia. This would make Piedmont-Sardinia the dominant north Italian state. The marriage arrangement would enhance the prestige of Napoleon's royal family.

■ *TIP* The pact was a major cause of the Franco–Austrian War (1859), which began the train of events resulting in the creation of the Kingdom of Italy (1861).

Pobedonostsev, Konstantin: a Russian politician in the reigns of *Alexander III* and *Nicholas II*, who introduced political repression following the assassination of *Alexander II* (1881).

- He limited the powers of the *zemstva* and introduced 'land captains' in 1892, to enforce the Tsar's will in the provinces.
- He organised *pogroms* against the Jews of Belorussia, introduced a system of *Russification* as an attempt to unite the empire, and set the *Okhrana* to arrest and detain political opponents.

■ *TIP* Pobedonostsev was a key figure in the conservative reaction in Russia from 1881 onwards.

pogrom: a government-backed attack on Jewish areas.

- Most closely associated with the *anti-Semitic* policies of *Tsar Alexander III* (1881–94), pogroms caused thousands of Russian Jews to emigrate to western Europe and the USA.
- The *Kristallnacht* ('Night of Breaking Glass') in Germany (1938) was also an example of a pogrom.

■ *TIP* Remember to use the term correctly. Not all attacks on Jews were pogroms.

Polish Corridor: the area of Polish territory between East Prussia and the rest of Germany, created by the Treaty of *Versailles* (1919).

● Under President *Wilson*'s *Fourteen Points*, the Allies were committed to creating an independent Poland with access to the sea. Therefore, although the Corridor had a mixed German and Polish population, it became part of the new Polish state.

● The predominantly German city of Danzig, adjacent to the Corridor, was made a 'free city' under the aegis of the *League of Nations*.

■ *TIP* Failure of the Polish government to agree to German demands for free access across the Corridor was the immediate cause of the German invasion in September 1939.

Polish Revolts, 1830–31, 1863: attempts to recreate an independent Polish state, which both failed.

● Until 1772 Poland had been a large eastern European state. During 1772–96 it was partitioned between Austria, Russia and Prussia.

● The revolts were put down mainly by Russia, but with assistance from the two other *Great Powers*.

● Although *Napoleon III* championed the cause of Polish nationalism, he failed to act in 1863 to support them.

■ *TIP* Fear of Polish nationalism helped to unite the three conservative eastern Great Powers of Austria, Russia and Prussia/Germany for much of the nineteenth century.

Politburo: the central decision-making body of communist Russia and the *USSR*.

● Roughly equivalent to the Cabinet in Britain, during *Lenin*'s rule the Politburo contained *Trotsky, Stalin, Bukharin, Kamenev* and *Zinoviev*.

● At the Tenth Party Congress in 1921 Lenin put forward the idea of 'democratic centralism'. Once the Politburo had agreed a policy, there could be no further discussion or debate in the Communist Party.

● Under Stalin, the Politburo simply endorsed his views.

Potsdam Conferences, July, August 1945: meetings of the USA, *USSR* and Britain at the end of the Second World War in Europe.

● It was agreed to make the German border with Poland the Oder–Niesse line. Reparations were discussed, with the USSR demanding 25% of reparations received from the Western Allied sectors, in addition to its own.

● The USSR agreed to enter the war against Japan.

● Controversially, large numbers of former Soviet citizens, who had fought with the Germans, were to be repatriated.

● The USA was represented by *Truman*, the USSR by *Stalin*. Britain was represented at the first conference by *Churchill*, who was replaced at the second by Clement Attlee, Attlee having led the Labour Party to victory in the July general election.

■ *TIP* The conferences failed to produce a long-term plan for the government of Germany. This led to major problems during the *Cold War*.

Prague, Treaty of, 1866: ended the Austro–Prussian War, by recognising Prussian dominance in Germany and Austrian withdrawal from German affairs.

● The *German Confederation* was abolished.

● Austria ceded Venetia to Italy. All the states in north Germany which had sided with Austria, except Saxony, were annexed by Prussia.

■ *TIP* This treaty fundamentally altered the *balance of power* in central Europe and paved the way for the unification of Germany under Prussia.

Prague Spring, 1968: an attempt to create a liberal communist regime in Czechoslovakia.

● Under the leadership of Alexander Dubček the Czechoslovak Communist Party introduced liberal reforms, such as the relaxation of censorship and granting greater powers to Parliament.

● The experiment was brought to an end in August 1968, when *Warsaw Pact* forces invaded Czechoslovakia.

● The Dubček regime was overthrown and traditional communist rule was reinstated under Gustav Husak.

■ *TIP* The Prague Spring was a forerunner of other liberal communist attempts at reform in the 1980s. The Soviet riposte was an early example of use of the *Brezhnev Doctrine*, aimed at preserving Soviet influence in east Europe.

Prairial, Law of 22nd, 1794: passed on 10 June (22 Prairial in the *Revolutionary Calendar*), allowing the Revolutionary Tribunal to leave evidence aside when trying a suspect.

● Judgement of acquittal or death could be made quickly. This led to a large increase in numbers executed in the *Terror* during the French Revolution. In June and July, 2,000 people were guillotined — more than the total for the whole of 1793.

● The law was forced through the *Convention* by *Robespierre*. Its impact was to force his opponents to take action, which they did on 27 July (9 Thermidor). Robespierre was arrested and subsequently executed.

■ *TIP* This measure unleashed the final part of the Terror, resulting in the fall of Robespierre.

Prohibition: US laws making it illegal to manufacture, sell or consume alcohol.

● National Prohibition was enacted through the Eighteenth Amendment and the Volstead Act. The latter defined intoxicating liquor.

● Known as the 'great experiment', Prohibition was widely ignored. 'Speakeasy' bars continued to sell alcohol. *Gangsters* made, and sold, alcohol across the USA.

● Because of the links to organised crime and the clear failure of enforcement, Prohibition came to an end in 1933. The Beer Act allowed the sale of beer and the Twenty-first Amendment to the Constitution reversed the Eighteenth Amendment, declaring that Prohibition was a state, not a federal, matter.

Quadruple Alliance, 1815: part of the second Treaty of Paris between Austria, Russia, Prussia and Britain and a continuation of the Fourth *Coalition against Napoleon* into peacetime.

- Under Article VI of the treaty, the four *Great Powers* agreed to meet from time to time to discuss the affairs of Europe.
- This formed the basis of the *Congress System*. In 1818, at the Congress of Aix-la-Chapelle, France was admitted, making it the Quintuple Alliance.
- *TIP* The Alliance embodied the spirit of European cooperation following the defeat of *Napoleon*.

Quebec Conference, 1944: meetings between *Churchill* and *Roosevelt* to draw up plans for the postwar division of Germany into occupation zones, and for the creation of an Allied Control Commission for Germany and Austria.

- They discussed the US Morgenthau Plan for the deindustrialisation of Germany after the war.
- Churchill offered Roosevelt use of the Royal Navy in the Pacific War against Japan.
- *TIP* This was part of US–British planning for the postwar world.

Quota 90: a decision to revalue the Italian lira, taken in 1927 by *Mussolini*.

- Following the First World War, the lira had gradually lost value against the pound sterling and had dropped to 127 lira per pound by 1927. Mussolini revalued it at 90 lira per pound.
- This gained Mussolini prestige in Italy, and with foreign financiers. However, the long-term effect on the economy was adverse. Overnight Italian exports became one and a half times as expensive as before, which hit the textile industry particularly hard. With the coming of the Depression (1929), the economic position was made worse.
- *TIP* The revaluation highlighted Mussolini's quest for prestige rather than long-term economic benefit.

RABKRIN: the 'Workers and Peasants' Inspectorate', set up in 1920 to investigate membership of the Russian Communist Party.

- *Lenin* believed the organisation was required because of the large increase in Communist Party membership since the *October Revolution* of 1917.
- *Stalin* was made Commissar. The post gave him the power to control membership of the party.

▮ *TIP* This position was used by Stalin to increase his power in the Communist Party, eventually allowing him to replace Lenin as Soviet leader.

Rasputin, Grigori: a Russian monk who influenced Tsar *Nicholas II* and the Tsarina, Alexandra.

- He established links with the Romanov royal family in 1905, when he claimed he could cure the Tsarevich (heir to the throne) Alexis of haemophilia. He hypnotised the child and Alexis's internal bleeding stopped.
- Following Nicholas II's decision to take personal command of the Russian armed forces (1915), in his absence Rasputin's influence over the Tsarina increased considerably. He was blamed by many supporters for undermining the government and was murdered by relatives of the Tsar in 1916.

▮ *TIP* Rasputin has been regarded as an important individual in undermining support for the tsarist regime in Russia. However, following his death, blame for the shortcomings of the Russian war effort were aimed directly at the Tsar. This led to his abdication in 1917.

Reagan, Ronald: US President (1981–89), known for his strong anti-communist views.

- In his first term (1981–85) he increased military spending and deployed Cruise and Pershing II missiles in Europe.
- He authorised an anti-communist intervention in the Caribbean island of Grenada (1983) and supported anti-communist Contra rebels in Nicaragua.
- He initiated development of the controversial Strategic Defence Initiative (*Star Wars*) anti-missile system, but in his second term (1985–89) negotiated with the Soviet premier, *Gorbachev*, for *Strategic Arms Reduction Talks* (START) on nuclear weapons.
- At home, he pursued a right-wing economic agenda which came to be known

r

as 'Reaganomics', introducing tax cuts and reductions in public spending which hit the poor.

- In 1986 he was affected by the Iran–Contra scandal, when his administration was accused of trading arms to Iran in return for the release of US hostages in Lebanon.

■ *TIP* Reagan was President during the 'New *Cold War*' of the early 1980s, but also helped pave the way for mutual arms reductions with the *USSR*.

Reconstruction Finance Corporation, 1932: established to lend $2 billion to rescue banks, insurance companies, railroads and construction companies in financial difficulties during the Depression.

- This was the most radical economic measure passed by *Hoover*'s Republican administration. It introduced the first direct federal aid to companies affected by the Depression.
- It was supplemented by the Emergency Relief and Construction Act of 1932, giving the Corporation the right to lend up to $1.5 billion to states to finance public works. Critics claimed it was too little, too late.

■ *TIP* Establishment of the Corporation was an important federal measure introduced during the *New Deal*.

Red Army: the army of the Soviet Union, created by Leon *Trotsky* during the Russian Civil War (1918–21).

redemption payments: made by Russian peasants following the *Emancipation of Serfs* (1861).

- Peasants had to pay for their freedom. However, payment was made for each village (*mir*) rather than for each peasant.
- The payments prevented peasants from leaving their villages, because this would increase the burden of payment on those who remained. They had the effect of preventing modernisation of the Russian economy.
- The payments were abolished in 1907 by *Stolypin*'s government.

■ *TIP* The payments caused much resentment among the Russian peasantry and helped foment unrest in the late nineteenth and early twentieth centuries.

Red Scare, 1919: a popular name for the fear of communism and socialism in the USA following the *October Revolution* (1917) in Russia.

- Industrial disputes were violently suppressed. Both the *Congress* and state legislatures passed laws banning socialist organisations.
- In 1920 'Palmer Raids' took place, when federal agents raided the Communist Party headquarters. Over 500 of those arrested were deported from the USA.

■ *TIP* Following the Russian Revolution, anti-immigrant feeling began to rise in the USA, which was manifested partly in the re-emergence of the *Ku Klux Klan* and the introduction of restrictions on immigration.

Reichsfeinde: a term used by *Bismarck* to describe those groups ('enemies of the state') he regarded as threats to the Prussian dominance of a united Germany after 1871.

- The term referred mainly to Catholics and Social Democrats. Catholics were feared because of their link to Polish nationalism in East Prussia, and because of their traditional support for Catholic Austria against Protestant Prussia. Social Democrats were feared because they supported a radical social, economic and political transformation of German society.

- Bismarck attacked German Catholics through the *Kulturkampf* anti-Catholic laws (1872–85).
- He attacked Social Democrats with anti-socialist laws from 1878 onwards. He was eventually dismissed (1890) by the Kaiser, *William II*, for advocating the introduction of martial law to crush the *Social Democrat Party*.

■ *TIP* The concept of Reichsfeinde helps to explain Bismarck's domestic policy between 1871 and 1890.

Reichstag: the lower house of the German National Parliament from 1871 to 1945.

- Under the Constitution of 1871 the Reichstag was elected by all males over 25 years of age.
- It possessed limited legislative power, but had the authority to pass the military budget every 7 years.
- As the one elected national institution, the Reichstag gained influence during the *Second Reich* (1871–1918).
- In *Weimar* Germany it was elected by both men and women through proportional representation (the percentage of votes cast was reflected in the percentage of seats acquired). Weimar governments required majority support in the Reichstag to survive.

■ *TIP* In the Second Reich the Reichstag was an important institution for representing German opinion. In Weimar Germany it formed the basis of democratic, parliamentary government.

Reichstag Fire, 1933: a key event in establishing *Hitler's* dictatorship.

- Communists were accused of burning down the National Parliament, as a prelude to an uprising. A Dutch communist was tried and executed for starting the fire.
- The fire was used by Hitler to pass a 'Decree for the Protection of the People and the State' the following day. It gave the government power to arrest at will, censor mail and search private houses.
- Most importantly, it gave Hitler power to take control of state (**Land**) governments if they failed to take measures to protect the security of Germany.
- President *Hindenburg* remained silent on the issue.

■ *TIP* The significance of the fire is that it allowed Hitler to persecute communists and tighten his grip on the reins of power.

Reinsurance Treaty, 1887: an agreement made between Germany and Russia following the collapse of the *Three Emperors' Alliance*, in which Germany supported Russian policy in the *Balkans*. More importantly, Germany was to stay neutral in a war between Russia and Austria-Hungary, providing it was not attacked.

r

- This was an attempt by *Bismarck* to remain an ally of both Austria-Hungary and Russia.
- It was to be renewed every 3 years. However, Bismarck's successor, von Caprivi, refused to renew the treaty in 1890, which ultimately led to the Franco–Russian Alliance (1893–94).
- ■ *TIP* This was part of Bismarck's system of alliances, which aimed to isolate France.

remilitarisation of the Rhineland, 1936: the sending of German troops into the Rhineland by *Hitler*, in contravention of the Treaties of *Versailles* and *Locarno*.

- Neither Britain nor France opposed the move, revealing their predisposition to a policy of *appeasement*.
- Remilitarisation greatly increased Hitler's popularity in Germany.
- ■ *TIP* This was the first attempt by Hitler to destroy the terms of the Treaty of Versailles. It was followed up by the *Anschluss* with Austria (March 1938) and the demand for the Czech *Sudetenland* to be incorporated into Germany (September 1938).

Rentenmark: a German currency introduced in 1923 in an attempt to end *hyperinflation*.

- It was introduced by Gustav *Stresemann*, but the idea was that of his Currency Commissioner, Hjalmar *Schacht*. As Germany did not possess sufficient gold reserves to back the new currency it was established with a mortgage on all German land and industry.
- The Rentenmark restored confidence in the currency until a new Reichmark was introduced (1924).
- ■ *TIP* Along with the *Dawes Plan*, the introduction of the Rentenmark helped to end the economic crisis of 1922–24.

reparations: payments made to the victors by a country defeated in war, to help pay for their costs of the war.

- Reparations are most closely associated with the Treaty of *Versailles* (1919). In Article 231 of the treaty, Germany accepted responsibility for causing the First World War and for all the damage wrought by the war.
- Reparations were decided by an Inter-Allied Reparations Commission which, in 1921, set the reparations figure at £6,600 million.
- This caused great resentment in Germany. It helped to generate *hyperinflation* in the German economy between 1922 and 1924. It also led to the Franco–Belgian occupation of the Ruhr (1923–24), when Germany temporarily failed to meet reparations payments.
- The *Dawes Plan* (1924) and the *Young Plan* (1929) were international agreements aimed at allowing Germany to pay reparations more easily.
- Reparations were cancelled in 1932, during the Depression.
- ■ *TIP* Reparations were an important cause of economic instability in *Weimar* Germany. They also contributed to the rise of extreme nationalist, anti-

democratic parties, such as the Nazis, who gained popularity by opposing the Treaty of Versailles.

Revolutionary Calendar: introduced in France in 1793 to replace the Christian calendar.

- The new calendar began on 22 September 1792, on the creation of the *First Republic*. 1792 became Year 1. Months were renamed according to the seasons such as Vendemaire, Brumaire and Frimaire for autumn, Nivose, Luviose and Ventoise for winter, Germinal, Floreal and Prairial for spring and Messidor, Thermidor and Fructidor for summer.
- Months were divided into three decades of 10 days each. Sundays and saints' days were scrapped.
- The new calendar was abolished by *Napoleon* in 1804.
- *TIP* The calendar reflected the desire for revolutionary change with the establishment of the First Republic.

Revolution of 1905: a major upheaval in Russia, which almost brought about the downfall of tsarism.

- It was caused by peasant unrest, defeat in the *Russo–Japanese War* (1904–05), and demands for social and political reform.
- It was a spontaneous revolution, sparked off by the 'Bloody Sunday' massacre in St Petersburg, where Russian troops dispersed a demonstration by factory workers demanding better conditions. It was characterised by a series of strikes, peasant *jacqueries* and mutiny in the Black Sea Fleet.
- Tsarism survived because the Army remained loyal, the revolutionaries were not united, and *Nicholas II* helped to split the opposition by issuing the *October Manifesto*.
- The main achievement of the revolution was the creation of a national parliament and the St Petersburg *Soviet*. The latter provided a model for the All-Russia Soviet of 1917.
- *TIP* The revolution showed the degree of resentment at tsarist rule. The underlying causes were only partly dealt with by Nicholas; the uprising proved to be a dress rehearsal for 1917.

Riga, Treaty of, 1921: ended the Russo–Polish War of 1920–21, the only attempt to export the *Bolshevik* Revolution, following a Polish attack on the Ukraine.

- The *Red Army* was defeated, mainly because the French gave military assistance to the Poles.
- The treaty gave a large area of western Belorussia to Poland, which was regained by the *USSR* as a result of the *Nazi–Soviet Pact* (1939).
- *TIP* This defeat ensured that the Revolution would be limited to Russia in the period immediately after the First World War.

Rights of Man and of the Citizen, 1789: a declaration by the French National Assembly, asserting 'natural rights' and the 'sovereignty of the people'.

- Natural rights included liberty, property, security and resistance to oppression, which led to equality before the law and in matters of taxation. It also

r

guaranteed freedom of speech and the press, and religious tolerance. However, the declaration did not include political or social equality. There was no mention of rights to education or help for the poor.

- Sovereignty of the people meant that the French were no longer subjects of the monarch, but free citizens.

■ *TIP* This was a revealing statement of the changes addressed by the moderate phase of the Revolution, 1789–91.

Risorgimento: a term describing the process of Italian unification (meaning 'resurrection').

- It was first used as a newspaper title by Count *Cavour* in 1847.
- The process encompassed nationalist revolution in 1830–31 and again in 1848–49. The chief drama began with the Franco–Austrian War of 1859 and *Garibaldi*'s expedition to Sicily and Naples in 1860.
- The Kingdom of Italy was declared in 1861, with its capital in Turin. In 1866 Venetia was added and the capital moved to Florence. In 1870 Rome became the capital. Finally, after the First World War, the South Tyrol and Fruilia were annexed by Italy.

■ *TIP* The Risorgimento was the chief liberal, national achievement of the mid-nineteenth century in Europe. It inspired the formation of the British Liberal Party in 1859.

Robespierre, Maximilien: the leading radical figure of the French Revolution.

- He led the Mountain (Montagnard) Party and rose to prominence when appointed to the *Committee of Public Safety* (1793).
- He presided over the *Terror* at its height and arrested and executed *Danton* and the *Hebertists*. He introduced the Festival of Reason and the Festival of the Supreme Being to replace religion.
- Robespierre was overthrown in the *Thermidorian Reaction* (July 1794), following the introduction of the Law of 22nd *Prairial*, which gave him sweeping powers of arrest.

■ *TIP* He was a controversial figure, credited both with saving the Revolution and introducing a personal dictatorship.

Rolling Thunder, Operation, 1965–68: the bombing of North Vietnam by the US Air Force.

- As a result of the *Tonkin Gulf Resolution* (1964) President *Johnson* was authorised to commit US forces to the *Vietnam War*. In addition to the bombing raids, ground troops were despatched to South Vietnam (1965). These events led to a major escalation of the war.
- Aerial bombing of the North continued until 1968, when Johnson announced his decision not to seek a second term as President.

■ *TIP* 'Rolling Thunder' failed to halt North Vietnamese support for the *Vietcong*, nor did it force them to the conference table to discuss peace.

Rome, Treaty of, 1957: created the *European Economic Community* (EEC) and Euratom.

- Signed by West Germany, France, Italy, Holland, Belgium and Luxembourg, the treaty was an important step towards European integration.
- It was a culmination of the *Schumann Plan* and superseded the European Coal and Steel Community.

■ *TIP* The treaty was the first in a series of developments, leading to the *Single European Act* (1986) and the *Maastricht Treaty* (1991), creating ever-closer European economic and political cooperation.

Rome–Berlin Axis, 1936: a term first used by *Mussolini* to describe a new, cordial relationship, following a series of agreements between Germany and Italy.

- A more formal treaty was not signed until 1939, the *Pact of Steel*.
- The axis marked a major reorientation of Italian foreign policy, following the invasion and conquest of *Abyssinia* (1935–36). Italy had previously joined the *Stresa Front* with Britain and France (1935), to oppose a German decision to reintroduce *conscription*.
- After 1936 Italy and Germany developed closer links. In 1937 they signed the *Anti-Comintern Pact* with Japan.

■ *TIP* This was a historic reversal of Mussolini's foreign policy.

Roosevelt, Franklin Delano: US President (1933–45), who led the USA out of the Depression and through the Second World War.

- The *New Deal* policies of 1933–41 mitigated the worst aspects of the Depression, bringing relief, recovery and reform. However, it was not until the outbreak of war in Europe (1939) that the US economy returned to prosperity.
- Roosevelt helped with Britain's fight against Germany from early 1941, by providing *lend-lease* aid. After US entry into the war (December 1941) he met with *Churchill* and *Stalin*, at Tehran (1943) and *Yalta* (1945), to discuss Allied strategy and its policy towards a defeated Germany. During the war he also gave the order to develop an atomic bomb.
- Elected to the presidency an unprecedented four times (1932, 1936, 1940 and 1944), he helped the Democratic Party to dominate US politics for a generation. He died in office in 1945, shortly before Germany surrendered.

■ *TIP* 'FDR' (as he was known) was a central figure in interwar American domestic politics and Second World War diplomacy.

rugged individualism: a US term to describe the need for self-reliance in social and economic matters.

- It was a central belief of the Republican Party in the interwar period.
- It reinforced the view that federal and state aid to help the unemployed would be both costly and unproductive. It also underlay the policy of laissez-faire, or free-market economics, whereby government intervention was regarded as potentially harmful to the economy.

■ *TIP* Presidents *Harding*, *Coolidge* and *Hoover* supported the idea (1921–33).

Ruhr Occupation, 1923–24: the occupation of the Ruhr industrial area by Belgian and French forces, in order to force Germany to renew *reparations*.

- The occupation was ordered by the French President, Poincaré, after the government in Germany had defaulted in the payment of reparations.

- Poincaré believed that the Germans had deliberately created an economic crisis to avoid paying reparations.
- Military occupation met with passive resistance, which deepened the economic crisis in Germany, resulting in *hyperinflation*.

TIP The occupation almost brought about the economic collapse of Germany and encouraged political extremism, such as the *Beer Hall Putsch* led by *Hitler* in November 1923.

Russell Dispatch, 1860: a statement by the British Foreign Secretary opposing any *Great Power* intervention in the Italian wars of unification.

- It prevented the intervention of France (1860), to stop *Garibaldi* crossing from Sicily to the Italian mainland.
- The British Liberal government had been formed in 1859, with a strong commitment to Italian unification.

TIP The dispatch enabled Garibaldi to invade and conquer Naples, a major factor in the creation of a united Italy (1861).

Russification: an attempt to increase unity in the Russian empire, through insistence on use of the Russian language in government, business and education.

- In the nineteenth century only half the empire was Russian-speaking. The policy was first introduced after the *Polish Revolt* of 1863, but is mainly associated with the reign of Tsar *Alexander III* (1881–94). The last part of the empire to face Russification was Finland, where Russian was not made the official language until 1900.

TIP Russification was generally regarded as a repressive policy by non-Russians.

Russo–Japanese War, 1904–05: a Far Eastern conflict, which resulted in a Russian defeat.

- In the 1890s the Russian government attempted to expand its influence into Manchuria, in northern China, and also Korea. It came into direct conflict with Japan, which had similar aims.
- War began with a Japanese surprise attack on the Russian Pacific Fleet in Port Arthur, Manchuria. The Russians were defeated on land at Mukden, in Manchuria, and at sea in the battle of Tsushima, between Korea and Japan.
- In the Treaty of Portsmouth (1905) Korea became an area of Japanese influence.

TIP This defeat was a contributory factor in causing the Russian *Revolution of 1905*. The war also emphasised the rise of Japan as a major Asiatic power.

SA (*Sturmabteilung*): a brown-shirted paramilitary 'stormtrooper' group, formed by the Nazi Party.

- Founded in 1921 under the leadership of Ernst Roehm, the SA provided protection for Nazi Party meetings and disrupted meetings of political opponents.
- Roehm and the SA leadership strongly supported the socialist, anti-capitalist ideas of the early National Socialist programme.
- With the SA swelling to a membership of 4.5 million, following *Hitler*'s rise to power, Roehm wanted it to replace the German armed forces.
- Seeing Roehm as a potential rival, and needing the support of the Army for his foreign policy plans, Hitler wiped out the SA leadership in the *Night of the Long Knives* (1934). After this the SA occupied a less prominent role in Nazi Germany.

■ *TIP* The SA constituted a powerful force in the rise of the Nazi Party. Its conflict with Hitler showed that the party was not completely united.

Sacco and Vanzetti Case: a US court case of the 1920s, which highlighted entrenched opposition to left-wing ideas.

- Two Italian immigrants with socialist ideas were arrested and tried for murder. Although the evidence was thin, both were sentenced to death.

■ *TIP* Along with the *Red Scare* (1919) and the Palmer Raids (1920), this piece of summary justice was an example of growing anti-immigrant and anti-left-wing feeling in the USA.

Sadat, Anwar: President of Egypt (1970–81) who, with Syria, launched the *Yom Kippur War* against Israel in 1973, failing to regain the Egyptian lands lost in the *Six Day War* (1967).

- In 1978 he completely changed Egyptian policy, signing the Camp David Peace Accord with the Prime Minister of Israel, Menachim Begin. Egypt recognised the state of Israel; the Sinai peninsula was returned to Egypt.
- The peace agreement caused resentment in the Arab world and within Egypt. Sadat was assassinated by his own troops in 1981.

■ *TIP* Sadat was the statesman who began the Middle East peace process.

SALT: see *Strategic Arms Limitation Treaties*.

Sammlungspolitik: the 'politics of bringing together', which was adopted by *William II*'s government from 1897 onwards, as a tactic to isolate the *Social Democrat Party* in the *Reichstag*.

- It equated to the domestic aspect of *Weltpolitik*, the German desire to create a large overseas empire and a large navy.
- *Weltpolitik* was supported by the right-wing and centrist parties. However, by 1909 the cost of naval building had grown to a point where extra taxation was required.
- The decision to increase sales tax split the **Sammlung** group of parties, alienating the Catholic *Centre Party*.
- ▨ *TIP* The failed attempt to limit the influence of the Social Democrats was compounded by the Reichstag elections of 1912, when the Social Democrats became the largest party, holding one-third of the seats.

sans culottes: a term to describe the mob, or crowd, in the French Revolution.

- Chiefly Parisian workers, they were the main supporters of the *First Republic* and the *Terror*.
- The term literally means 'without breeches', signifying that they wore the trousers of manual workers, not the clothing of high society. They comprised a wide variety of occupations, from skilled workers and shopkeepers to manual labourers. In 1792–94 they numbered approximately 500,000 out of the Paris population of around 700,000.
- Their main concerns were the cost of living and the huge gap in wealth between rich and poor.
- ▨ *TIP* This was the central group in the development of the Revolution from its moderate to its radical stage.

San Stefano, Treaty of, 1878: ended the Russo–Turkish War (1877–78), but caused international uproar by creating a new, large, Slav state in the *Balkans* — Bulgaria.

- The treaty also gave territory to Russia in southern Bessarabia and the Caucasus.
- Both Serbia and Montenegro were enlarged at Turkey's expense.
- Austria and Britain threatened war with Russia over the treaty. The international crisis was solved with a meeting of the *Great Powers* at the Congress of Berlin, which produced the Treaty of *Berlin* (1878).
- ▨ *TIP* The treaty was regarded as a victory for Russian *pan-Slavs*, but heightened tensions in the *Eastern Question*.

Sarajevo: capital of Bosnia and scene of the assassination of Franz Ferdinand (1914), which was the immediate cause of the outbreak of the First World War. It led to the *July Crisis*.

- It was also the setting for a siege between Serbs, Muslims and Croats during the Bosnian Civil War in the early 1990s. The city suffered a 2-year siege by Bosnian Serbs, until relieved by *UN* security forces.
- It is now the capital of the independent state of Bosnia-Herzegovina.

TIP Sarajevo highlights the political instability of the western *Balkans* at the beginning and end of the twentieth century.

Schacht, Hjalmar: Currency Commissioner in Germany under *Stresemann* (1923), President of the Reichsbank (1933–37) and Minister for the Economy (1934–37).

- An influential figure in economic policy, Schacht introduced the *Rentenmark* in 1923, which stabilised the German currency and ended *hyperinflation*.
- In the 1930s he was credited with the Nazi economic miracle of rapidly reducing unemployment between 1933 and 1936. He devised a means of acquiring valuable raw materials without immediate payment.

TIP Schacht's resignation in 1938 marked a radical new phase in *Hitler's* policies.

Schengen Agreement, 1985: made between seven members of the *European Union*, concerning the abolition of border controls from 1995 onwards.

- France, Holland, Belgium, Luxembourg, Germany, Italy, Greece, Spain and Portugal created a single border zone.
- The aim was to control more effectively the influx of illegal immigrants and coordinate the fight against crime. It heralded an important step towards European integration.
- Britain refused to join and has kept control of its own borders. Concern over illegal immigrants, the smuggling of illegal drugs and the need to keep out rabies influenced this decision.

TIP This is a good example of the increase in political integration within the Union during the 1980s, when Jacques Delors was President of the EU Commission.

Schlieffen Plan: the German war plan, in existence from 1905 to 1914, which was based on the belief that a future war would involve Germany in fighting both France and Russia.

- Recognising that France would mobilise its army much faster than Russia could, von Schlieffen, the Chief of the Army General Staff, planned to attack France first, defeat it, and then move the German Army east to confront Russia. As speed was essential to the success of the plan, it was decided to outflank France by attacking through Belgium.
- In August and September 1914 the plan almost worked. However, the German Army was halted just north of Paris, in the first Battle of the *Marne*.

TIP The plan put pressure on German diplomats to act quickly during the *July Crisis*. When Russia mobilised its army on 30 July, Germany was forced to implement the plan on 1 August. But the decision to go through Belgium brought Britain into the war on France's side.

Schönbrunn, Treaty of, 1809: made between France and Austria, following Austria's defeat at the Battle of Wagram.

- Austria lost 3.5 million subjects and had to pay a large war indemnity. Its army was restricted to 150,000 men.

- Salzburg was given to Bavaria, the Illyrian Provinces to France, and parts of Galicia to Russia and the Grand Duchy of Warsaw.
- Austria was forced to join the *Continental blockade* against Britain.
- **TIP** The treaty marked the height of *Napoleon*'s influence in Europe. It also saw *Metternich* replace Stadion as Austrian Foreign Minister. Metternich was to play a major role in the defeat of Napoleon from 1812 onwards.

Schuman Plan, 1950: a scheme which united the coal and steel industries of France, West Germany, Italy, Holland, Belgium and Luxembourg in the European Coal and Steel Community.

- This was the forerunner of the *European Economic Community*, created in 1957.
- However, attempts to create a European Defence Community between 1950 and 1954 failed. Western Europe continued to rely on *NATO* for defence.
- **TIP** This early step in west European integration arose from a concern that Germany's coal and steel industries should never again be employed to attack its neighbours.

Scramble for Africa, 1880–1914: the rapid partitioning of most of Africa not already under colonial control, which was part of the *new imperialism*.

- Africa was carved up between Britain, France, Spain, Portugal, Italy, Belgium and Germany.
- The most rapid period of colonial expansion took place following the Berlin West Africa Conference (1884–85). The speed of colonisation was partly fuelled by a fear of missing out on acquiring colonies.
- The scramble produced the only crises of the period between European powers, notably the *Fashoda Incident* (1898) between Britain and France, and the *Moroccan Crises* (1905 and 1911) between Germany and France.
- **TIP** The scramble was part of a general spread of European influence and control across the globe in the late nineteenth century.

SD (*Sicherheitsdienst*): the Security Service of the *SS* in Nazi Germany, created in 1932 under the leadership of Reinhard *Heydrich*. In 1939 the Reich Security Head Office was created, which controlled the *Gestapo* and the SD.

SEATO: see *Southeast Asia Treaty Organisation*.

Second Empire in France, 1852–70: created when Louis Napoleon, President of the Second Republic, proclaimed himself *Napoleon III*, heir to the empire of *Napoleon*.

- He regarded his father, the Duke of Reichstadt, as being Napoleon II, although the Duke never ruled France.
- The empire can be divided into three distinct phases, an authoritarian period up to 1860 when Napoleon III ruled as a dictator, a liberal period to 1869 when some political activity was tolerated, and a parliamentary period (1869–70) when Napoleon III became a constitutional monarch.
- The empire was characterised by a desire to make France, once again, Europe's major power. It was overthrown by France's defeat in the *Franco–Prussian War* (1870–71).

▪ *TIP* This brought the Napoleonic dynasty to an end and was the last period of monarchical rule in France.

Second Reich, 1871–1918: the German empire created by *Bismarck* following the German wars of unification, which was dominated by Prussia and ruled by the Hohenzollern family.

● With a strong army, an industrialised economy and a growing population, the Second Reich had the potential to dominate Europe.

● Only under Kaiser *William II* did Germany embark on a policy (*Weltpolitik*) which attempted to create a global colonial empire. *Weltpolitik* created international tension between the *Great Powers* and resulted in closer cooperation between Britain, France and Russia, and fear in Germany of encirclement.

● The Second Reich was also characterised by a rise in popularity of the *Social Democrat Party*, which was seen as a threat to the social and political structure by successive German governments.

● The internal and external problems facing Germany by 1912 forced the German government to risk war to solve its problems. Instead, the First World War resulted in a revolution, which overthrew the empire in November 1918.

▪ *TIP* The problems of the Second Reich were a dominant theme in European affairs from 1871 to 1918.

Second Republic in France, 1848–52: created following the overthrow of King *Louis Philippe* in the *February Revolution of 1848*.

● It initially followed socialist policies, such as the establishment of *National Workshops*, but the republic became more moderate following the *June Days* uprising of 1848. Its short life can be explained by the election of Louis Napoleon as President in December 1848.

● Louis Napoleon was determined to become a permanent ruler and overthrew the democratic constitution in a coup (1851). One year later he declared the creation of the *Second Empire* with himself as Emperor *Napoleon III*.

▪ *TIP* Questions often concentrate on why the republic was short-lived.

September Massacres, France, 1792: the killing in Paris of between 1,500 and 2,000 prisoners, thought to be supporters of the monarchy.

● There were a variety of reasons for the massacres, such as fear of military defeat at the hands of Austria and Prussia following the fall of Longwy and the siege of Verdun, and the desire of the *Commune* to terrify voters to secure a majority in the *Convention*.

▪ *TIP* The massacres were part of a radical move to the left in the Revolution. Soon afterwards the Convention replaced the Legislative Assembly, and this was followed swiftly by proclamation of the *First Republic*.

serfdom: a social system in which agricultural labourers and domestic servants were the personal property of their owners.

● It was the dominant social system in medieval Europe, but was confined to eastern Europe, particularly Russia, by the late eighteenth century.

- This was seen as a major threat to the dominance of the Prussian landowning class, and successive German governments between 1871 and 1914 attempted to limit the influence of the party.
- It formed the first democratic government following the German revolution of 1918 and remained one of the largest political parties in *Weimar* Germany.
- Abolished under *Hitler*, the party re-formed after the Second World War to become a major force in West German politics.
- **TIP** The SPD was viewed as the major internal threat to the *Second Reich* and its rise was a factor in the German decision to risk war in 1914.

socialism in one country: the conviction that communism should be established in the Soviet Union first, before being exported to other countries.

- It was associated with *Stalin* and his supporters, in the period following *Lenin*'s death.
- It ran counter to the view of *Trotsky,* who supported the idea of *permanent world revolution*. This was an important reason why Stalin, instead of Trotsky, replaced Lenin as leader. By the mid-1920s Russia had suffered a decade of world war, revolution, civil war and famine. The country was not in a position to spread communism abroad.
- **TIP** Questions on communist Russia frequently require an understanding of basic communist ideology.

Social Revolutionaries: a political group in Russia, formed in 1902 by Victor Chernov, which supported the peasantry.

- They believed in a 'peasant revolution' creating a socialist society of workers and peasants, in which the village community (**mir**) would be preserved.
- They received only limited representation in the second *Duma* before the First World War, but became the largest party following the Constituent Assembly elections in 1917.
- The more radical members joined *Lenin*'s *Bolshevik* Party in a coalition after October 1917, but left following the signing of the Treaty of *Brest-Litovsk* in March 1918. Social Revolutionaries attempted to overthrow the Bolsheviks.
- **TIP** They were an important revolutionary group in Russia during the first two decades of the twentieth century.

Social Security Act, 1935: introduced federal old age pensions, widow and widower benefits, unemployment benefit and specific aid for the blind and dependent children.

- Passed during the second *New Deal*, the act marked the birth of a federal welfare system with the creation of the Social Security Administration.
- It became the basis of the US welfare system until 1996.
- **TIP** This was one of the lasting achievements of the New Deal and, with the creation of the *Works Progress Administration* and the *Wagner Act*, a central feature of the second New Deal.

Solidarity: a Polish independent trade union movement formed in 1980, which posed a major threat to communist rule in Poland.

- It began as a result of a strike in the Lenin Shipyard at Gdansk and spread rapidly across Poland, leading to the fall of Edvard Gierek as the Polish communist leader.
- Solidarity was led by a former plumber, Lech Walesa. It demanded official recognition as a non-communist organisation.
- In 1981 the Polish Prime Minister, General Jaruzelski, banned Soldarity, introduced martial law and arrested its leaders. Jaruzelski's actions forestalled a Soviet intervention, but failed to quash support for Solidarity.
- Following the fall of communism in 1989 Walesa was elected President of Poland under its first democratic government.
- **TIP** Solidarity was an important rallying point for undermining communism in eastern Europe.

Somme, Battle of, 1916: a failed attempt by British and French armies to break the deadlock on the Western Front during the First World War.

- Promoted as General Haig's 'Big Push', the first day of the battle proved disastrous for the British Army, which suffered 60,000 casualties.
- The battle lasted from July to November, with little gain.
- It was also important as the scene for the first use of tanks.
- **TIP** The Somme battle epitomised warfare on the Western Front, with mass infantry attacks on entrenched positions defended by artillery and machine guns.

Southeast Asia Treaty Organisation (SEATO), 1954: comprising the USA, Britain, France, Australia and New Zealand, the Philippines, Thailand and Pakistan, and part of *Eisenhower*'s policy of encircling the communist world with military alliances.

- Its formation followed the end of the French phase of the *Vietnam War* and the creation of communist North Vietnam. South Vietnam later became an associate member. SEATO obligations were used by the USA to justify its military involvement in South Vietnam and Laos.
- **TIP** Less powerful than *NATO*, SEATO was nonetheless a key alliance in the *Cold War* and for bolstering US involvement in Vietnam.

soviet: literally a 'council', but used in Russia to describe elected bodies of soldiers, workers and peasants.

- The original model was the St Petersburg Soviet (1905), chaired by Leon *Trotsky*.
- Mainly linked with the Russian Revolutions of 1917, soviets formed spontaneously in the Army and among workers and peasants, following the fall of Tsar *Nicholas II*.
- Initially the *Petrograd* (St Petersburg) Soviet, and then the All-Russia Soviet, acted as an alternative government to the *Provisional Government*. *Lenin* used *Bolshevik* support in the Soviet to legitimise his seizure of power in the *October Revolution of 1917*.
- **TIP** German revolutionaries set up 'soldiers' and workers' councils'. These were the equivalent of soviets in the Russian context.

Spanish Civil War, 1936–39: a conflict between the democratically elected socialist/communist government and the Spanish armed forces and nationalists under *Franco*.

- It began following a Popular Front victory in parliamentary elections. The Spanish Army attempted a coup, which led directly to war.
- The nationalists were supported by fascist Italy and Nazi Germany and the Republican government was supported by the *USSR* and communist groups across Europe.
- British and French neutrality was an important factor in ensuring the eventual victory of Franco.

▪ *TIP* The war was significant as a prelude to the Second World War in Europe.

Spartacist Uprising, 1919: a communist attempt to overthrow the *Weimar Republic* led by Karl Liebknecht and Rosa *Luxemburg*.

- The Spartacists (German communists) attempted to seize Berlin in a manner similar to the *Bolshevik* seizure of *Petrograd* in October 1917.
- The attempt failed, mainly because the *Social Democrat* government of Friedrich *Ebert* used the *Freikorps* to suppress the revolt. Both Liebknecht and Luxemburg were murdered.
- The uprising split the left wing in Weimar Germany. The Spartacists formed the German Communist Party (KPD) in 1918, which competed with the Social Democrats for the working-class vote.

▪ *TIP* Though unsuccessful, the revolution revealed the political instability which blighted the early years of Weimar Germany.

SPD: see *Social Democrat Party of Germany*.

splendid isolation: a term to describe the period of British foreign policy between 1856 and 1902, when Britain remained aloof from formal international alliances.

- By 1894 the other four European *Great Powers*, Russia, France, Germany and Austria-Hungary, were in formal military alliances.
- Britain instead formed specific agreements on individual issues, such as the partition of Africa, with other European states.
- Britain's diplomatic isolation became an issue only during the *Boer War* (1899–1902). This led to the formation of the *Anglo–Japanese Alliance* (1902), Britain's first military alliance since the *Crimean War*.

▪ *TIP* The term is usually used to describe Lord Salisbury's foreign policy between 1885 and 1902.

Squadristi: black-shirted Italian *fascist* paramilitary groups.

- They mainly comprised ex-soldiers, who were anti-socialist and nationalist.
- In 1919 and 1920 they attacked trade unionists and socialist organisations, chiefly in central Italy. Intimidation of socialists aided *Mussolini*'s rise to national prominence. The Fascist Party was seen as the only serious opponent of the Italian Left.
- Squadristi participated in the *March on Rome* (1922), which resulted in Mussolini becoming Prime Minister. Once he was in power, the Squadristi were renamed

the Militia for National Security and assisted Mussolini in creating a fascist dictatorship in 1925.

■ *TIP* The use of violence, and the threat of it, were tools used by Mussolini in his rise to power.

SS (*Schutzstaffel*): literally, a protection squad — *Hitler*'s élite force.

● Under the leadership of *Himmler*, the SS destroyed the leadership of the *SA* in the *Night of the Long Knives* (1934).

● The SS organised and administered the concentration camp system and the *Final Solution*.

● Following the German invasion of the *USSR*, the SS administered large areas of occupied territory in the Ukraine and the Baltic States.

● During the Second World War the Waffen (armed) SS formed the élite forces of the German Army and contained recruits from Germany, France, Holland and other occupied states. At its height, the strength of the Waffen SS was over 2 million men.

■ *TIP* The SS comprised a state within a state in the Nazi empire.

Stakhanovite Movement: an attempt to increase industrial production through propaganda during the Second *Five Year Plan* in the *USSR*.

● It began in 1935 and was named after Alexsei Stakhanov who, it was said, mined 102 tonnes of coal in one shift.

● Stakhanov was hailed as a hero of Soviet labour, and other workers were encouraged to emulate him. The movement became unpopular among workers, as production targets were forced up.

● Under *Gorbachev*'s *glasnost* (openness) policy (1985), Stakhanov's achievement was shown to be fraudulent.

■ *TIP* The movement was an example of *Stalin*'s use of propaganda in an attempt to raise industrial production.

Stalin, Joseph: ruler of the Soviet Union (1924–53), who rose to power through his control of the Communist Party.

● He became a member of the *Politburo* (1917), head of *RABKRIN* (1919), and General Secretary of the party (1922).

● He began the 'Second Russian Revolution' with the introduction of forced *collectivisation* and rapid industrialisation after 1928.

● To quell opposition, he initiated the Great *Purge* (1934–39). By 1941 he was responsible for the deaths and imprisonment of tens of millions of Soviet citizens.

● He successfully led the *USSR* through the Second World War, making it one of the two superpowers by 1945.

● He extended communism to eastern Europe and encouraged the spread of communism in Asia, aiding North Korea in the *Korean War* (1950–53). By the time of his death in 1953 the USSR was a nuclear power.

■ *TIP* Stalin was one of the dominant world statesmen of the twentieth century. He transformed the USSR into an industrialised superpower.

Stalingrad, Battle of, 1942–43: a critical German defeat on the Eastern Front in the Second World War.

- In the final phase of the German offensive to capture oilfields and the Caucasus region of southern Russia the German VIth Army, under General von Paulus, was surrounded by the *Red Army*, under General *Zhukov*, in Stalingrad on the River Volga. After a bitter battle the beleaguered Germans were forced to surrender. Four hundred thousand men were taken prisoner.
- This battle was regarded as the turning-point on the Eastern Front.
- **TIP** Stalingrad began a major retreat of the German Army from eastern Ukraine and the Caucasus.

START: see *Strategic Arms Reduction Talks*.

Star Wars, 1983: a plan put forward by President *Reagan* as a way of making the USA immune to a nuclear missile attack.

- Named Star Wars after a series of popular science fiction films, the programme's proper title was the Strategic Defence Initiative (SDI). It involved advanced laser technology, located in satellites, to shoot down incoming missiles.
- It created considerable tension between the USA and the *USSR*. Negotiations in Reykjavik, Iceland, in 1986 failed to produce agreement on nuclear disarmament.
- The USA was unable to test the technology for the implementation of SDI. However, continued interest in the project at the end of the twentieth century led to a significant renewal of the nuclear arms race with the USSR and communist China.
- **TIP** Plans for the programme were a destabilising feature of the *Cold War* in the 1980s.

Stavka: headquarters of the Russian Army in both world wars.

- In the First World War *Nicholas II* was at Stavka headquarters at Mogilhev when the *February Revolution* (1917) broke out in *Petrograd*. His inability to return to Petrograd because of a railway strike helped to force his abdication.
- In the Second World War Stavka was based at the Kremlin under the direct control of *Stalin*.

Stolypin, Peter: Russian Prime Minister (1906–11), who introduced land reform and a restricted right to vote in the *Duma*.

- He hoped to preserve tsarism by creating a class of independent peasants.
- He used Article 87 of the *Fundamental Law* to issue decrees when the Duma was not sitting.
- In 1907 he issued a law restricting the right to vote to the wealthier classes. This meant that the third and fourth Dumas contained far smaller numbers from left-wing parties.
- In 1908 he made a declaration that compulsory education for all would be introduced within 10 years. He was assassinated by a *Social Revolutionary*.
- **TIP** Stolypin's reforms were a serious attempt to modernise the Russian countryside while maintaining the political system largely unchanged. His premature death ended a brief period of reform.

Straits Convention, 1841: an international agreement by the five *Great Powers* on the Straits of the Dardanelles and the Bosphorus, which separate the Black Sea from the Aegean.

- It declared that the Straits were to be closed to warships of all nations and reversed the terms of the Treaty of *Unkiar Skelessi* (1833).
- It was a triumph for the British Foreign Secretary, Lord *Palmerston*, who prevented Russian warships from entering the eastern Mediterranean.

■ *TIP* This was a good example of the *Concert of Europe* in operation.

Strategic Arms Limitation Treaties (SALT), 1972, 1978: agreements between the USA and *USSR* to limit the growth of nuclear weapons.

- In 1972 the limitation centred on anti-ballistic missile (ABM) systems.
- Because of the Soviet invasion of Afghanistan in December 1979 the second SALT treaty was not ratified by the US Senate.
- As a result, a new *Cold War* developed in the early 1980s.

■ *TIP* The treaties were an important aspect of *détente* between the USA and USSR in the 1970s.

Strategic Arms Reduction Talks (START): an initiative of President *Reagan* in 1982, designed to begin the reduction, rather than just limitation, of nuclear weapons.

- Talks were suspended in 1983 following the US deployment of Cruise and Pershing II missiles in Europe (*intermediate nuclear forces* or INF).
- An INF treaty was signed in 1987 and in 1991 *Gorbachev* finally agreed to sign a START treaty with President *Bush*, in return for economic aid. Each superpower was limited to 1,600 missiles and 6,000 warheads, with a plan to cut nuclear arsenals by 30%.

■ *TIP* The START treaty marked the final episode in the *Cold War*, being signed shortly before the collapse of the *USSR*.

Stresa Front, 1935: agreements made between Britain, France and Italy, which condemned the reintroduction of conscription and rearmament in Germany, both of which broke the Treaty of *Versailles*.

- Cooperation was undermined, however, with Britain signing the Anglo–German Naval Agreement in June and by the Italian invasion of *Abyssinia* in October.

■ *TIP* The weakness of the front helps to explain why international attempts to stop *Hitler* proved unsuccessful.

Stresemann, Gustav: Chancellor (1923) and Foreign Minister (1923–29), who led Germany out of the economic crisis of 1922–24 by ending passive resistance in the Ruhr (1923), introducing the *Rentenmark*, and supporting the *Dawes Plan*.

- He was founder (in 1919) and leader of the German People's Party, successor to the National Liberal Party.
- In 1925 he signed the *Locarno Treaty*, accepting Germany's western borders as determined by the Treaty of *Versailles*.

- He negotiated German entry into the *League of Nations* (1926) and accepted the *Young Plan* (1929) for the rescheduling of reparations, shortly before his death.
- ■ *TIP* He was the most accomplished statesman of the *Weimar Republic* during the 1920s. His premature death deprived the moderates of a leader just before the Depression.

Sudetenland: an area of western Czechoslovakia which contained 3.5 million German speakers.

- It was the crux of the *Munich Crisis* (1938), when *Hitler* demanded its incorporation into Germany. The Sudetenland Germans were led by Konrad Henlein, who supported Hitler's plan.
- Loss of the Sudetenland deprived Czechoslovakia of its western defences, making further German annexation of territory much easier.
- ■ *TIP* It is essential to refer to the Sudetenland when describing or explaining the Munich Crisis.

Suez Crisis, 1956: an international crisis caused by Egyptian nationalisation (take-over) of the Suez Canal.

- It led to an Egyptian–Israeli war and Anglo–French military intervention to reverse the Egyptian action.
- The military campaign was condemned by both the USA and *USSR*. British and French troops were forced to withdraw because of international opposition.
- The fiasco was a humiliation for the British Prime Minister, Anthony Eden.
- ■ *TIP* This was the last attempt by Britain and France to act as independent colonial powers in the Middle East.

Supreme Court: the highest court of appeal in the United States, with the power to interpret the US Constitution.

- The court consists of nine judges appointed for life by the President, with the consent of the Senate.
- In the 1930s the Supreme Court declared large parts of the first *New Deal* unconstitutional. *Roosevelt*'s attempt to change the composition of the court (1937) met with widespread opposition.
- In the 1950s, 60s and 70s, under Chief Justice Earl Warren, the Supreme Court made several judgements which greatly assisted the African American *civil rights* movement. The *Brown v. Board of Education Case* (1954) was an important landmark in school desegregation.
- ■ *TIP* An understanding of the power of the Supreme Court is essential to a study of American history.

Taft–Hartley Act, 1947: an anti-trade union act, passed over President *Truman's* veto by a conservative *Congress*.

- The act outlawed the trade union 'closed shop' and allowed the federal government to impose a 'cooling-off' period of 30 days before a strike could take place.
- It modified the pro-trade union *Wagner Act* (1935).
- **TIP** The act illustrates the problems Truman had with a conservative majority in Congress, made up of Republicans and Southern Democrats.

Talleyrand, Charles: French politician, statesman and Foreign Minister (1797–1807), who helped to create the *Confederation of the Rhine* (1806) and attended the Congress of Vienna (1814–15) as representative of King *Louis XVIII*.

- He secured recognition for France as a *Great Power* and worked closely with Britain to limit the territorial demands of Prussia and Russia.
- **TIP** He was an important participant at the Vienna Congress.

Tannenberg, Battle of, 1914: a key German victory on the Eastern Front, which halted the Russian invasion of East Prussia at the beginning of the First World War.

- It brought to national prominence Generals *Hindenburg* and *Ludendorff*. The victory was consolidated by a second Russian defeat at the Battle of the Masurian Lakes.
- Towards the end of 1914 another victory at the Battle of Lodz led to a Russian retreat from East Prussia and Russian Poland.
- **TIP** As happened with other military leaders, the battles made heroes of Hindenburg and Ludendorff. The failure of Russian arms also encouraged Tsar *Nicholas II* to take personal command of the Russian armed forces (1915), with catastrophic results.

Tehran Conference, 1943: the first meeting of the 'Big Three' (*Stalin, Roosevelt* and *Churchill*) during the Second World War.

- They discussed the opening of a Second Front in western Europe, which eventually occurred with the *D-Day* landings in northern France (1944).
- They also discussed the possible entry of the *USSR* into the war with Japan, and the need to create a postwar peacekeeping organisation.

- As a result of the conference, Churchill came to mistrust Stalin. By contrast, Stalin and Roosevelt worked well together.
- *TIP* The conference saw the beginnings of Britain's decline as a world power. It heralded the rise of two superpowers, the USA and USSR.

Tennessee Valley Authority, 1933: a substantial achievement of the '100 Days' of the first *New Deal*.

- Building dams on the Tennessee River prevented soil erosion and provided electricity through hydroelectric power for a large part of the upper South of the USA.
- The project encouraged the development of industry, such as aluminium smelting.
- *TIP* This was a good example of cooperation between federal and state governments during the Depression.

Tennis Court Oath, 1789: a declaration by representatives of the Third Estate that they would not disperse until a French constitution was created and firmly established.

- This occurred after the Third Estate had taken the name 'National Assembly' and had been excluded from the Hall of the Estates.
- *TIP* This action was a critical move in precipitating the French Revolution.

Terror, French Revolutionary, 1792–94: the period when the government of France resorted to mass arrests and executions to stay in power.

- It was caused largely by fear of defeat in the French Revolutionary War against Austria and Prussia, a major economic crisis and counter-revolutionary uprisings in western France.
- It was most closely associated with the work of the Revolutionary Tribunal, the *Committee of Public Safety* and the Committee of General Defence.
- Its chief characteristic was public execution by guillotine. Approximately 13,000 people were executed.
- It reached its height in 1793–94 under *Robespierre* and came to an end with Robespierre's overthrow (1794).
- *TIP* The Terror was the most important feature of Robespierre's period of ascendency in the French Revolution. It was the main reason why conservatives and moderates were much more influential in the Republic after the mid- 1790s.

Test Ban Treaty, 1963: an agreement between the USA, *USSR* and Britain to ban nuclear tests in the earth's atmosphere.

- It was the result of growing concerns about the effects of radioactive fall-out, following the nuclear tests of the 1950s. It led to rising public anxiety, and in Britain to the formation of the Campaign for Nuclear Disarmament (CND).
- The three signatories agreed to conduct underground nuclear tests only.
- The treaty did not apply to France; nor did communist China recognise the ban. China exploded its first nuclear device in 1964.

■ *TIP* An example of East–West *détente* following the *Cuban Missile Crisis*, this was the first international agreement to limit tests on nuclear weapons.

Tet Offensive, 1968: an attempt by the *Vietcong* to launch a national communist revolution against the South Vietnamese government during the *Vietnam War*.

- All major towns and cities across South Vietnam were attacked and the US embassy in Saigon was temporarily occupied. US forces at Khe Sanh suffered a 50-day siege by the North Vietnamese Army, before being relieved.
- Although the communist attacks were defeated, they secured a major political and propaganda victory. The US commander, General Westmoreland, demanded 200,000 extra troops and suggested calling up the army reserve. President *Johnson* refused.

■ *TIP* The offensive was an important factor in persuading Johnson not to seek re-election as President in 1968. It also fuelled growth of the antiwar movement in the USA.

Thatcher, Margaret: Britain's first woman Prime Minister (1979–90), and the first since Lord Liverpool, in the early nineteenth century, to win three successive general elections.

- She was a strong opponent of the *USSR* and a close ally of President *Reagan*. Known by the Soviets as the 'Iron Lady', she supported the US deployment of Cruise missiles in Britain in 1983.
- She recovered the Falkland Islands, following the Argentine invasion of 1982.
- In domestic affairs, she introduced privatisation and tackled growth in the size of the public sector. She defeated a major strike by the coal miners (1984–85) and signed an agreement with the Republic of Ireland over Northern Ireland (1985).
- Increasingly, Thatcher became a critic of Britain's role in the *European Union*, which led to her downfall in 1990.

■ *TIP* She was the most influential British politician in the last quarter of the twentieth century.

Thermidorian Reaction, 1794–95: the overthrow of *Robespierre* and the *Jacobins* and the end of the Revolutionary *Terror*.

- Following enactment of the Law of 22nd *Prairial*, Robespierre had power to arrest and execute at will. In a meeting of the *Convention* (1794) he threatened any opponent with arrest. Although backed in the *Commune*, Robespierre failed to rally wider support, which led to his arrest and execution.
- Following the fall of Robespierre, the powers of the *Committee of Public Safety*, the Commune and the Revolutionary Tribunal were greatly reduced.
- The final defeat of the Jacobins came with suppression of the risings on 12th Germinal (April) and 1st Prairial (May) 1795.

■ *TIP* The reaction inaugurated a moderate phase in the Revolution, which saw establishment of the *Directory*.

Thiers, Adolphe: a French politician and journalist who played an important role in the 1830 and 1848 Revolutions and the Paris *Commune of 1871*.

- As a journalist, he helped to bring down King *Charles X* and supported the claim of *Louis Philippe*.
- He was made Foreign Minister in 1840 and supported *Mehemet Ali* in the Eastern Crisis, bringing confrontation with Britain and his own dismissal by the King.
- In the *February Revolution of 1848* he persuaded Louis Philippe to leave Paris, and became a prominent opposition MP from 1863 during *Napoleon III*'s rule.
- He became the first President of the Third Republic (1871–73) and negotiated the Treaty of *Frankfurt* with Prussia/Germany (1871). He also suppressed the Paris Commune (1871).
- **TIP** Thiers was an important political figure across four major changes in regime between 1830 and 1871. He represented moderate liberalism in France.

Three Emperors' Alliance, 1881–87: an international agreement between Germany, Austria-Hungary and Russia, which was set up by *Bismarck* following the collapse of the *League of the Three Emperors* in the *Great Eastern Crisis* (1875–78).

- The three powers agreed to stay neutral if one of the signatories went to war with a fourth power.
- Austria-Hungary and Russia also acknowledged each other's sphere of influence in the *Balkans*.
- **TIP** This was a continuation of Bismarck's policy of keeping France isolated. However, the *Bulgarian Crisis* (1885–87) rekindled Austro–Russian tensions in the Balkans. The Alliance was to be renewed every 3 years, but Austria-Hungary refused to renew it in 1887, which led to the Russo–German *Reinsurance Treaty* (1887–90).

Tiananmen Square massacre, 1989: a violent suppression in Beijing of Chinese students' demands for political change during and after *Gorbachev*'s visit to China.

- Gorbachev's liberal reforms of *glasnost* (openness) raised expectations of liberal change across the communist world.
- In China the propensity for change was also helped by the 'Four Modernisations' programme of *Deng Xiao Ping*.
- Although the Chinese leaders were keen on liberal economic reforms, they were against relaxation of Communist Party control. The protests were crushed by Premier Li Peng, using the Chinese Army.
- **TIP** The repression resulted in international condemnation of China and the worsening of US–Chinese relations during the *Bush* presidency.

Tilsit, Treaty of, 1807: an agreement between *Napoleon* and Tsar *Alexander I*, which ended the war of the Third *Coalition against Napoleon*.

- Prussia lost all its territory west of the River Elbe, and Westphalia was made a kingdom under Napoleon's brother, Jerome.
- The Grand Duchy of Warsaw was created, France received the Ionian Islands and Alexander also recognised Napoleon's recently established states in Italy, Holland and Germany.

- In a secret part of the treaty, Napoleon urged Russia to take Finland from Sweden, and Moldavia and Wallachia from the *Ottoman* (Turkish) *empire*.
- ■ *TIP* The treaty marks the beginning of a period of European dominance by Napoleon, which lasted until 1812.

Tito, Josip: a statesman who liberated Yugoslavia (1945) and established the Federal Communist Republic, becoming Prime Minister (1945–53) and President (1953–80).

- He led the communist partisans against German and Italian occupation during the Second World War (1941–45), but fell out with *Stalin* (1948) and had Yugoslavia expelled from *Cominform*.
- He then formed an independent communist state and later became a leader of non-aligned states, which were allies of neither the USA nor the *USSR*.
- His death in 1980 began a process of disintegration, with Yugoslavia breaking up into a number of warring states.
- ■ *TIP* He maintained political stability in the western *Balkans* for most of the *Cold War*.

Tonkin Gulf Resolution, 1964: a decision by *Congress* to give President *Johnson* authority to deploy US forces in the *Vietnam War*.

- It resulted from an incident in the Gulf of Tonkin off North Vietnam, where two US destroyers were allegedly attacked by North Vietnamese torpedo boats in international waters.
- Johnson used the resolution to bomb North Vietnam in Operation *Rolling Thunder* (1965) and to commit ground troops to South Vietnam later that year.
- ■ *TIP* The resolution led to what has been described as the 'imperial presidency', where limited wars were fought by US troops overseas without any formal declaration of war by Congress.

Trafalgar, Battle of, 1805: a major naval victory by Britain over the combined forces of France and Spain.

- Under Admiral Lord Nelson, the Royal Navy split the French and Spanish battle line.
- Although Nelson was killed in action, the British victory prevented a French invasion of Britain. It also gave the Royal Navy supremacy at sea, which it retained throughout the nineteenth century.
- ■ *TIP* The victory enabled Britain to break the *Continental blockade* and supply both its forces in the *Peninsular War* (1808–14) and its allies in the Fourth *Coalition against Napoleon* (1812–14).

Triple Alliance, 1882: a secret military alliance between Germany, Austria-Hungary and Italy, an expansion of the *Dual Alliance* (1879).

- Italy wished to join the Dual Alliance following the French acquisition of Tunis (1881), on which Italy had designs. Germany offered potential support in a war between Italy and France.
- The Alliance consolidated *Bismarck*'s attempt to isolate France diplomatically. It was renewed every 3 years until 1914.

- However, in 1902 Italy signed a secret alliance with France, which contradicted the Triple Alliance. Friction also developed with Austria-Hungary over Italy's claim on the unredeemed lands of South Tyrol and Istria in Austria-Hungary. On the outbreak of the First World War Italy remained neutral, ultimately joining Britain and France (1915).

▨ *TIP* The Alliance was an important aspect of European diplomacy, 1882–1914.

Troppau, Congress of, 1820: the second European congress following the Treaty of *Vienna* (1814–15).

- It was notable for acceptance of the Troppau Protocol by four of the *Great Powers*, Russia, Prussia, France and Austria, which claimed the right to intervene in the internal affairs of any European country to suppress liberal revolution.

- The Protocol was opposed by Britain with a Diplomatic Note (1820), claiming that the Great Powers had a right to intervene in the internal affairs of European states only if the *balance of power* was threatened.

▨ *TIP* This was the first real rift between the Great Powers since the defeat of *Napoleon*, and led to the break-up of the *Congress System*.

Trotsky, Leon: a leading Russian communist, who came to prominence as chair of the St Petersburg *Soviet* during the *Revolution of 1905*.

- He became chair of the *Petrograd* Soviet and joined the *Bolsheviks* (1917), organising the Bolshevik seizure of power in the *October Revolution*.

- As *Commissar* for Foreign Affairs, he negotiated the Treaty of *Brest-Litovsk* with Germany and Austria-Hungary (1918).

- As Commissar for War, he founded the *Red Army* during the Civil War (1918–21) and suppressed the *Kronstadt Mutiny* (1921).

- He worked with *Lenin* in 1923 to prevent *Stalin* from succeeding to power, but was ousted by Stalin, *Kamenev* and *Zinoviev* in 1924–25. He was exiled in 1929 and assassinated by a Stalinist agent in Mexico City (1940).

▨ *TIP* Trotsky supported the idea of *permanent world revolution* rather than *socialism in one country*.

Truman, Harry: US President (1945–53), who introduced the *Truman Doctrine* and *Marshall Aid* (1947) and led the Western Allies in the *Berlin Airlift Crisis* (1948–49) and the *Korean War* (1950–53).

- He succeeded Franklin D. *Roosevelt* to the presidency, authorising use of the *atomic bomb* against Japan.

- His aggressive, 'Give 'em hell' philosophy led to a serious deterioration in relations with the *USSR* and he was criticised by Republicans for losing China to communism (1949) and for dismissing General MacArthur, the US commander in Korea.

- At home, attempts to introduce social reform in the 'Fair Deal' programme were thwarted by a conservative alliance of Republicans and Southern Democrats in *Congress*, but he achieved desegregation of the US armed forces (1948).

■ *TIP* Truman's belligerence towards the Soviet Union is regarded as an important factor in causing the *Cold War.*

Truman Doctrine, 1947: the announcement of the policy of *containment.*

● Following the *Long Telegram* (1946), the *Truman* administration decided to adopt an aggressive foreign policy towards the *USSR* by supporting anti-communist forces.

● It was first used to effect in the *Berlin Airlift Crisis* (1948–49) and later in the *Korean War (*1950–53).

● Containment became a key feature of US *Cold War* policy. It involved the establishment of *NATO, SEATO* and *CENTO,* and also support for non-communist governments across the world — even if they were undemocratic.

■ *TIP* This was one half of Truman's policy of containment; the other was *Marshall Aid.*

Ultras: extreme conservatives in the Bourbon Restoration in France (1814–30).

- They favoured a return to the absolute monarchy of the *ancien régime* and were supporters of the Comte d'Artois during the reign of *Louis XVIII* (1814–24).

- When the Comte d'Artois became *Charles X* (1824), the Ultras gained considerable influence. The power of the Catholic Church increased and religious orders were allowed to return to France. The press was censored and the National Guard abolished. These changes were epitomised by the ministry of Prince Polignac (1829–30) and led to demands for political reform, which resulted in the *July Revolution* of 1830.

■ *TIP* Make sure that you use the term for the Bourbon Restoration. 'Ultra' can mean different things at other times and in other states.

UN: see *United Nations (Organisation)*.

Union of Unions: an organisation for political reform set up during the *Revolution of 1905* in Russia.

- Formed by Paul Miliukov, leader of the *Kadets*, it brought together 14 national unions of professionals, including lawyers, teachers, writers and doctors.

- It included the Union for Jewish Equality and for the Equality of Women, a Union of Railway Employees and a Union of *Zemstvo*-Constitutionalists.

- As the Revolution progressed the Union of Unions became more radical, supporting the strike movement. In order to prevent collapse of the state, Tsar *Nicholas II* agreed to the *October Manifesto*.

■ *TIP* The Union of Unions helped to extract the promise of political change made by the Tsar.

United Nations (Organisation) (UNO): an international organisation created in 1945 to replace the *League of Nations*.

- It took over several of the League's agencies, such as the International Labour Organisation and care for refugees.

- It also contained agencies for education and culture, but its main aim was to help preserve peace.

- Unlike the League, the UN was empowered to use troops in a peacekeeping role, but they had to be provided by member states. Peacekeeping troops have operated in many parts of the world, including Cyprus, the Middle East, Bosnia, Sierra Leone and, most significantly, the *Korean War* (1950–53).

- The organisation is dominated by the Security Council, of which the USA, *USSR*, Britain and France were original permanent members. Communist China became a member in 1972.
- By the year 2000 the original 51 members of the UN had risen to 185.
- ■ *TIP* Based in New York, the UN has failed to prevent the outbreak of wars across the globe since 1945. However, it has assisted in establishing and maintaining peace following several conflicts.

Unkiar Skelessi, Treaty of, 1833: an agreement between Russia and the *Ottoman* (Turkish) *empire*, which ended the first *Mehemet Ali* crisis of 1831–33.

- A defensive alliance between the two countries, whose most controversial aspect was a secret article allowing Russia to close the Straits (of the Dardanelles and the Bosphorus) at will. This gave Russia considerable influence over the Ottoman empire and naval operations in the Mediterranean.
- It was opposed by the British Foreign Secretary, Lord *Palmerston*, who aimed to reverse the terms of the treaty. In 1838 Palmerston concluded an Anglo–Turkish Convention, which established free trade between the countries.
- In the second Mehemet Ali crisis (1839–41), Britain intervened to help the Ottoman empire. This resulted in the *Straits Convention* (1841), which reversed the Treaty of Unkiar Skelessi.
- ■ *TIP* The treaty was an aspect of the *Eastern Question* which greatly increased British suspicions of Russian intentions in the Middle East.

unrestricted U-boat warfare: the German naval tactic of seeking to create an economic blockade around Britain during the First World War.

- By the end of 1916 the blockade was only partially successful. Germany then announced that any shipping, including neutral shipping, would be sunk if it entered an exclusion zone around the British Isles.
- Seen as a violation of the freedom of the seas, the decision had the effect of bringing the USA, and several Latin American states, into the war against Germany. The tactic almost worked by the end of 1917, but the introduction of rationing and the convoy system limited its effects.
- ■ *TIP* The decision by Germany to attempt a blockade changed the course of the First World War.

USDP: see *Independent Social Democrats*.

USSR, 1922–91: the 'Union of Soviet Socialist Republics', created by *Lenin* as a way of dealing with the question of nationalities within the communist-controlled state.

- Almost half the population of the territory ruled by the *Bolsheviks* was non-Russian. Lenin established a union of separate republics, including Russia, the Ukraine, Belorussia and Transcaucasia. After the Second World War this was expanded to include 15 republics.
- Even within a republic there were autonomous regions of self-government,

such as the Chechen–Ingushetia Autonomous Republic in Russia. However, all republics were ruled over by the Communist Party.

- Following the fall of communism (1991), the USSR disintegrated into separate national units.

■ *TIP* The USSR was the only country without a geographical limitation in its title. The aim was for the whole world to be part of the USSR eventually.

Valmy, Battle of, 1792: a crucial victory for French Revolutionary forces over Prussia.

- Under the leadership of Dumouriez, the French used artillery to great effect to win this important victory. Later the same year Dumouriez defeated the Austrians at Jemappes.
- Both victories saved France from invasion and with it, the French Revolution. The French then invaded Belgium, the Rhineland and Italy.

■ *TIP* Occurring at the time of the declaration of the *First Republic*, this was an important early turning-point in the French Revolution.

Varennes, flight to, 1791: an attempt by *Louis XVI* to flee France and join up with Austrian forces in Belgium.

- Louis XVI and his family were captured by a band of peasants and led back to Paris.
- Louis's flight led to a rise in anti-monarchist feeling and the appearance of the first Republican clubs, such as the Cordelier. However, following the massacre in the Champs de Mars (1791) the Cordelier Club was disbanded.

■ *TIP* Louis XVI lost considerable support and was forced to accept the *Constitution of 1791*.

VC: see *Vietcong*.

Velvet Revolution, 1989: the overthrow of communist rule in Czechoslovakia, following its collapse in East Germany.

- In November the Berlin Wall was opened, allowing free movement between East and West Berlin. Street demonstrations took place in the Czech capital, Prague, organised by Civic Forum, an opposition group.
- With the collapse of communism occurring in Hungary, Poland and Bulgaria, the Czech Communist Party gave way to allow dissident writer, Vaclav Havel, to become head of the government.

■ *TIP* This was a clear example of how peacefully and quickly communist rule collapsed in eastern Europe in 1989. Without the backing of the Soviet Army, the communist government found it had little popular support.

Verdun, Battle of, 1916: one of the major battles on the Western Front during the First World War.

- Attempting to bleed the French Army of reserves by attacking a key point in its defensive line, the German commander, von Falkenhyn, led a year-long siege, in which both sides lost over 100,000 men.
- The French prevented the capture of Verdun, but at great cost. Von Falkenhyn's failure led to his removal and replacement by Generals *Hindenburg* and *Ludendorff*.
- **TIP** The battle typified warfare on the Western Front. Mass infantry attacks were used, but were thwarted by artillery. The stalemate continued until the summer of 1918.

Verona, Congress of, 1822: the last major conference of the *Congress System*.

- It attempted to reach agreement on some intervention to end the Spanish liberal revolution of 1820, and also revolutions in Latin America against Spanish rule.
- The Russian Tsar, *Alexander I*, offered to suppress the Spanish revolution with a Russian Army of 15,000, but this was opposed by the other *Great Powers*, notably France. The congress broke up, without agreement. The French eventually intervened in Spain (1823) to depose the revolutionary government.
- The new British Foreign Secretary, *Canning*, appointed following the suicide of Castlereagh, refused to attend.
- **TIP** The congress marked the end of the Congress System. Canning favoured the *Concert of Europe*, but would not support intervention to suppress liberal revolution.

Versailles, Treaty of, 1919: an agreement between Germany and the Allies, in which Germany was forced to accept responsibility for starting the First World War.

- Germany was also held responsible for all damage and costs of the war, known as *reparations*, set at £6,600 million (1921).
- German military power was greatly reduced. It lost its High Seas Fleet and its air force; the Army was reduced to 100,000 men.
- A demilitarised zone was created in the Rhineland on the Franco–German border. Germany also lost territory to France, Poland, Denmark, Belgium and Lithuania (over 10% of national territory) as well as its entire overseas empire.
- **TIP** The treaty caused considerable resentment in Germany. It helped to undermine German democracy, established in 1918, and greatly assisted the rise of *Hitler*.

Vichy France, 1940–44: the area of France which had a pro-German government under the leadership of Marshal Pétain, following the fall of France (1940) in the Second World War.

- France was split in two. Northern and western France were placed under direct German military control. Central and southern France were placed under a right-wing government, with its capital at Vichy.
- The administration introduced anti-socialist and *anti-Semitic* laws. From November 1942 it was occupied by German forces, but collapsed following the *D-Day* landings in northern France (1944).

■ *TIP* For the period 1940–44, the French were split in their allegiance between the 'Free French' under *de Gaulle*, who fought with the Allies, and the Vichy French, who supported Germany.

Vienna, Treaty of, 1814–15: an agreement which brought the Napoleonic Wars to an end.

● It redrew the map of Europe, creating a *balance of power* between the five *Great Powers* of Britain, France, Austria, Russia and Prussia.

● Britain received Malta, the Cape of Good Hope, Heligoland, Mauritius and Ceylon.

● Prussia received Westphalia and two-fifths of Saxony.

● Russia received Finland, Poland and Bessarabia.

● Austria received Venetia, but lost the Austrian Netherlands.

● A defensive barrier (the **cordon sanitaire**) was placed around France. This included the United Netherlands, Prussia and an enlarged Piedmont-Sardinia.

■ *TIP* The treaty prevented war between the Great Powers until the *Crimean War* (1853–56), but it re-established conservative governments, helping to precipitate liberal revolution in 1820–21, 1830–31 and 1848–49.

Vietcong (VC): volunteer communist *guerrilla* fighters, who fought both the South Vietnamese and American forces in the *Vietnam War*.

● They controlled large areas of South Vietnam and often operated at night. During the day they became farmers or workers.

● They attempted to mount a national communist revolution in the *Tet Offensive* (1968). It failed and American forces destroyed the Vietcong command structure temporarily.

● After the Tet Offensive the North Vietnamese regular army took most of the responsibility for fighting the Americans and South Vietnamese.

■ *TIP* Do not confuse the Vietcong with the Vietminh (see next entry).

Vietminh: a Vietnamese nationalist organisation dominated by communists and established in 1941 by *Ho Chi Minh*.

● It initially fought the French and the Japanese (1941–45), but then fought a war of independence against the French (1946–54). It succeeded in creating the independent communist state of North Vietnam, following the *Geneva Accords* (1954).

● During the 1960s and early 1970s it was renamed the National Liberation Front, because it was attempting to unite North and South Vietnam.

■ *TIP* The Vietminh was the main Vietnamese nationalist organisation, 1941–54.

Vietnamisation: a policy introduced by President *Nixon* to reduce the number of US ground troops in South Vietnam.

● From 1969 onwards the USA gradually withdrew its troops, instead giving training and modern equipment to the South Vietnamese Army.

● The South Vietnamese succeeded in halting the North's Spring Offensive in 1972, supported by massive US aerial bombing, allowing Nixon to sign a peace agreement in 1973 (withdrawing all US ground forces) to fulfil his pledge of 'peace with honour'.

V

- However, the South Vietnamese Army collapsed under a further attack by the North, which overran the country in 1975.
- **TIP** Together with improving diplomatic relations with the *USSR* and communist China, Vietnamisation was the centrepiece of Nixon's foreign policy, supported by massive aerial bombing of North Vietnam.

Vietnam War, 1946–75: a series of wars to create an independent, communist-controlled Vietnam.

- Between 1946 and 1954 the *Vietminh* fought the French colonial forces, which were defeated at the Battle of *Dien Bien Phu*. The French pulled out and North and South Vietnam became separate countries.
- From 1956 to 1964 communist *guerrillas* in South Vietnam fought the South Vietnamese government.
- From 1965 to 1973 a large number of US troops supported the South Vietnamese government, together with massive aerial bombardment of North Vietnam and guerrilla forces in the South by the US Air Force.
- In 1975 South Vietnam was invaded and conquered by the North.
- **TIP** The Vietnam War was the greatest conflict of the *Cold War* in Asia. It also created deep divisions in American society and led to large antiwar demonstrations.

Villafranca, Peace of, 1859: ended the Franco–Italian War of 1859 and was made by the French Emperor, *Napoleon III*, without consulting his ally, Piedmont-Sardinia.

- It came about only after bloody French victories at Magenta and Solferino.
- France was given the Austrian province of Lombardy, which it passed on to Piedmont-Sardinia. Napoleon III failed to meet his obligation to free northern Italy from Austrian control.
- **TIP** The Peace led to the temporary resignation of *Cavour* as Prime Minister of Piedmont-Sardinia.

Volksgemeinschaft: an attempt by the Nazis to create a classless society of Germans (a 'folk community') based on racial purity.

- Youth organisations such as the *Hitler Youth* and the League of German Maidens, together with the *Kraft durch Freude* ('Strength through Joy') organisation, were part of the programme designed to achieve it.
- It was hoped that this development would end social conflict between capital and labour. The new enemies of Germany would be Jews, gypsies and communists.
- **TIP** The Nazi domestic social programme was largely an attempt to attain a 'folk community'.

Wagner Act, 1935: a measure guaranteeing American workers the rights of collective bargaining through trade unions of their own choice during the second *New Deal* (also known as the Wagner–Connery Act).

- It created a three-man National Labor Relations Board, to ensure a fair outcome to industrial and wage disputes.
- Employers were forbidden to discriminate against trade unions.

■ *TIP* This was a major landmark in labour relations in the USA. It gave unions federal recognition, but was later watered down by the *Taft–Hartley Act* (1947). Although the act was passed during *Roosevelt*'s presidency, he was, at best, only mildly in favour of it.

Wall Street Crash, 1929: the financial collapse of the New York Stock Exchange (located in Wall Street), which sparked a world-wide economic depression.

- The stock market collapse was due to overspeculation in stocks and shares, with speculators securing shares by paying a 10% deposit in the expectation that share prices would rise, providing them with a profit.
- A sudden collapse in prices on the New York Stock Exchange left thousands of people with debts they could not meet, leading ultimately to the collapse of banks and economic depression.
- US company decisions to withdraw their overseas investments also fuelled the German economic collapse.

■ *TIP* It has been regarded as the immediate cause of the Depression. However, there was already overproduction in the US economy. The crash highlighted weaknesses in the economies of the USA and the rest of the industrial world.

Wannsee Conference, 1942: a Nazi meeting which launched the *Final Solution* to the Jewish question.

- Led by *SS* General Reinhard *Heydrich*, it laid out a plan to exterminate Europe's Jews.
- Up to the time of the conference, Polish Jews were confined to ghettoes in cities such as Warsaw, Lodz and Krakow. The conference planned to exterminate these ghettoes with the construction of *death camps* at Auschwitz, Sobibor, Treblinka, Maidanek and Belzec. Later, Jews from the other occupied territories would be exterminated.

- The conference was attended by officials from the Ministry for the Occupied Eastern Territories, the German Foreign Office, the General Government of Poland, the Reich Chancellery, and the Race and Resettlement Office.
- **TIP** This was an important landmark in the Final Solution (also known as the Holocaust), which transformed random murder into systematic extermination.

War Cabinet Meeting, 1912: a meeting of the German Emperor, *William II*, with his senior military and political advisers, where it was decided to risk starting a European war to solve Germany's foreign and domestic problems.

- By 1912 the *Social Democrat Party* was the largest in the *Reichstag* and its left-wing leanings threatened the political and social structure of the German empire.
- The failure of *Weltpolitik* to secure a large overseas empire had backfired and led to the encirclement of Germany by Britain, France and Russia.
- **TIP** The meeting is now regarded by many historians, including Fritz Fischer, Immanuel Geiss and Volker Berghahn, as an important cause of the First World War.

war communism: the *Bolshevik* economic policy (1918–21) which was introduced during the Civil War in Russia and involved state control of industrial production.

- Elite groups of 'storm workers' were formed, which were used to improve vital war production.
- It also involved grain procurement to feed the cities, whereby Red Guards forcibly took grain from the peasants as it was harvested.
- By 1921 this policy had led to a drastic decline in economic growth and famine in the Russian countryside. It was replaced at the Tenth Party Congress by the *New Economic Policy*.
- **TIP** This was an early and unsuccessful attempt to introduce a centrally directed economic policy. Similar methods were used after 1928 by *Stalin*.

War Guilt Clause: Article 231 of the Treaty of *Versailles* (1919), which declared that Germany and its allies were responsible for the outbreak of the First World War.

- It caused outrage in Germany, but the exhausted nation had no option but to accept the treaty.
- The clause helped *Hitler* and other extreme nationalists to gain support.
- It was strenuously denounced in Germany and, as memories of the war receded, the German view received growing support in the West, leading to the policy of *appeasement*.
- Since 1961 the writings of German historians such as Fritz Fischer have reopened the debate on German responsibility for starting the war.
- **TIP** The issue was a festering sore in German politics after 1919.

War in Sight Crisis, 1875: a crisis engineered by *Bismarck*, in response to French inability to pay off the war debt (indemnity) of the *Franco–Prussian War* (1870–71).

- Bismarck and the German General Staff feared the re-emergence of French military power and supported the idea of a preventive war against France.
- The crisis began with a German newspaper article, produced with Bismarck's blessing, entitled 'Is war in sight?'.
- Plans for a preventive war were halted when Britain and Russia protested at German actions.

■ *TIP* This was an early setback for Bismarck's foreign policy after 1871. It showed that other *Great Powers* were willing to set limits to changes to be countenanced in the European *balance of power*.

Warsaw Pact, 1955: a military alliance between the *USSR* and its Eastern allies, which was the Communist Bloc equivalent of *NATO*.

- The agreement was signed following the West German announcement of rearmament and its decision to join NATO.
- Although ostensibly directed against the West, the pact gave the USSR increased military control over its satellites. It was used to suppress the *Prague Spring* in Czechoslovakia (1968).

■ *TIP* The pact was a key military alliance of the *Cold War* in Europe. From 1955 to 1989 Europe was split into two military alliances, each on constant war alert.

Warsaw Uprising, 1944: the destruction of the Polish 'Home Army' by German forces in the latter stages of the Second World War.

- Following the victory of the *Red Army* in Operation *Bagration*, Soviet forces reached the east bank of the River Vistula in the summer of 1944, a few miles from Warsaw.
- The secret Polish Home Army seized the moment to rise up against the German occupation, in order to create a nationalist Polish government before the Red Army arrived.
- After initial successes, the uprising failed because the *USSR* refused to intervene to support the Poles. After a month's fighting, the Home Army was destroyed along with much of Warsaw.
- The USSR created a new Polish government made up entirely of communists, known as the Lublin Committee, in Soviet-occupied Poland.

■ *TIP* The replacement of one oppressor by another created considerable bitterness in Poland and among the Western Allies. *Stalin* had effectively removed a possible threat to future communist rule in Poland.

Watergate Scandal, 1972–74: a political scandal which forced the resignation of President *Nixon* in the USA.

- It was caused by Nixon's use of unconstitutional methods for financing and conducting his re-election campaign to the presidency in 1972. Anxious about what his opponents knew, he authorised a break-in at the Watergate building, headquarters of the Democratic opposition.
- Attempts by *Congress* to investigate claims of irregular election methods were blocked by Nixon, claiming executive privilege.

W

- Eventually Nixon's position was undermined by his legal counsel testifying to a Senate committee and by the discovery that Nixon had taped all his White House conversations. Federal and *Supreme Court* demands led to the hand-over of most of the tapes.
- Nixon's attempt to lie his way out of the scandal eventually led to a vote in favour of impeachment (dismissal) by the Senate, which forced Nixon to resign.
- **TIP** This was a key episode in US domestic affairs during the decline of the 'imperial presidency'.

Waterloo, Battle of, 1815: the final defeat of *Napoleon* by the combined forces of Britain and Prussia.

- Napoleon's return from exile on Elba in early 1815 led to the final 'Hundred Days' of Napoleonic rule in France.
- Attempting to invade Belgium, the French Army was eventually stopped south of Brussels. A French victory seemed assured until the appearance of the Prussian Army under General Blücher, late in the afternoon.
- The defeat led to the second exile of Napoleon, this time on the south Atlantic island of St Helena, and to the second Treaty of Paris between France and the Allies.
- **TIP** The battle prevented a further phase of European warfare and established the Duke of Wellington's reputation as a military commander.

Weimar Republic, 1918–33: a period of German democracy between the wars, founded on the German revolution of 1918 when the Emperor, *William II*, abdicated and went into exile in Holland.

- The Republic was undermined through its association with the Treaty of *Versailles* (1919). It faced attempts to overthrow it from right and left between 1919 and 1923.
- It was also hampered by the economic crisis of 1922–24.
- The Republic collapsed following the Depression (1929–33), which saw the rise of both the Nazi and Communist parties, and finally came to an end on the appointment of *Hitler* as Chancellor in January 1933.
- **TIP** German democracy was never firmly established. Many historians think it was doomed to fail from the start.

Weltpolitik: the German strategy of 'world politics' (1897–1914), in which Germany aimed to become a colonial power alongside Britain and France.

- It was to be achieved through building a large navy and acquiring an overseas empire.
- Seen as a natural progression in the development of German history, it was also based on a belief in *Social Darwinism*, which encouraged the view that Germany must become a world power because the Germans were a superior race.
- Attempts to build a large overseas empire met with very limited success. The Caroline and Marianas islands were seized, but the building of a large navy antagonised Britain, where it was seen as a threat. The search for colonies pushed Britain, France and Russia closer together.

- After 1909 *Weltpolitik* was modified to encompass **Mitteleuropa**, the aim being to dominate Europe first and then acquire an overseas empire.
- **TIP** This policy was a leading cause of the deterioration in European relations before the First World War.

White Rose Movement: an opposition movement to *Hitler*, which organised protests against Nazi atrocities.

- It was founded in 1943 by Hans and Sophie Scholl and based at Munich University. Arrested for distributing anti-state literature, the Scholls and their associates were hanged.
- **TIP** This was one of very few examples of overt opposition to the Nazi regime beyond the armed forces.

William I: King of Prussia (1858–88) and German Emperor (1871–88), whose attempt to modernise and enlarge the armed forces led to a confrontation with the Liberals in 1862.

- He succeeded Frederick William IV and appointed *Bismarck* Minister-President to deal with the Liberal crisis in the Prussian *Landtag* (Parliament).
- Bismarck ignored the *Landtag* and increased the size of the Army.
- William I supported Bismarck's aggressive foreign policies, which led to war with Denmark (1864), Austria (1866) and France (1870–71).
- He accepted the position of German Emperor from his fellow monarchs at Versailles in January 1871 and supported Bismarck's policies between 1871 and 1888.
- He survived two assassination attempts in 1878.
- **TIP** He had the power to dismiss Bismarck at any time, but accepted his minister's policies.

William II: the third German Emperor (1888–1918), who came into conflict with *Bismarck*, launched *Weltpolitik* and *Sammlungspolitik* and was forced to abdicate at the end of the First World War.

- He followed the short reign of his father, Frederick III, which lasted for a few months only.
- An arch-conservative with a volatile personality, he wanted to rule as well as reign. This led to conflict with Bismarck, whom he dismissed in 1890 because the Chancellor wanted to introduce martial law to nullify the influence of the *Social Democrat Party*.
- Following a brief interlude when von Caprivi and von Hohenlohe were Chancellors, he launched *Weltpolitik* and *Sammlungspolitik*, aiming to preserve Prussian control of Germany while creating a large overseas empire.
- He accepted the German decision to go to war in 1914, but was forced to abdicate in 1918 following the revolution. He fled to Holland, where he died in 1942.
- **TIP** He was a policy maker in Germany from the mid-1890s onwards and thus an important figure in causing the First World War.

Wilson, Woodrow: US President (1913–21), who was a major world statesman in the final stages of the First World War and the *Paris Peace* Conference that followed it.

- In January 1918 his *Fourteen Points* peace proposal became the 'unofficial' war aim of the Allies.
- At the Paris Peace Conference in 1919 he supported the idea of *national self-determination* as the basis of achieving world peace. He also supported the idea of the *League of Nations*.
- Wilson returned disappointed to the USA after the conference because Britain and France had forced through a harsh peace on Germany. The Treaty of *Versailles* was not ratified (supported) by the US Senate.
- He suffered a stroke in 1920.
- **TIP** Wilson is a major figure in any discussion of the Allied victory in the First World War and the peace settlement that followed it.

Witte, Sergei: Finance Minister (1892–1903) and Prime Minister (1905–06), whose principal achievements were the rapid industrialisation of Russia in the early 1890s and 1900s, and publication of the *October Manifesto*.

- Industrialisation was driven by his organisation of the building of the Trans-Siberian Railway. He used French loans to finance the enterprise.
- Dismissed in 1903 because of opposition from the Russian armed forces, Witte returned to power as a result of the *Revolution of 1905*. He persuaded the Tsar to issue the October Manifesto, but was dismissed again in 1906, following introduction of the *Fundamental Law*, to be replaced by *Stolypin*.
- **TIP** He began the modernisation of late tsarist Russia and helped to save the Tsar in the 1905 Revolution.

Works Progress Administration, 1935: an organisation for recruiting the unemployed to sign up to public works projects during the second *New Deal*.

- By 1941 it had become the largest employer in the USA, with 2 million employees (20% of the work-force).
- The administration was not allowed to compete directly with private firms or to build houses. However, it built 1,000 airports, 8,000 schools and hospitals and 12,000 playgrounds.
- Under the leadership of Harry Hopkins, it aimed to get the unemployed back to work — any work — and was created under the Emergency Relief Appropriation Act.
- **TIP** This was an enormous New Deal agency and shows the extent of government involvement in the economy.

X, Malcolm: an African American political activist of the 1960s.

● He changed his name from 'Little' to 'X' because he refused to be known by a slave name.

● He was brought up in the North of the United States and spent much of his early years involved in criminal activity. He was sent to prison, where he converted to the Islamic faith.

● He first supported the creation of a separate Black nation within the USA, but later broke with the 'Nation of Islam' movement and set up his own more moderate organisation in 1964.

● He was assassinated by gunmen from the Nation of Islam in Harlem, the African American ghetto in New York City.

■ *TIP* Malcolm X stands in marked contrast to Martin Luther *King*. He promoted a more militant policy for African American advancement.

Yalta Conference, 1945: a meeting of the three 'Big Three' (*Stalin*, *Roosevelt* and *Churchill*) held in February to discuss policy towards Europe following the defeat of *Hitler*.

- Disputes centred on the future government of Poland. Stalin gained agreement that lands lost to Poland by the *USSR* in the *Treaty of Riga* (1921) should be returned. In compensation, Poland would receive land from Germany, including part of East Prussia and Silesia.
- They agreed to establish the *United Nations* to replace the *League of Nations*.
- As an interim measure, Germany and Austria were to be divided into four military zones of occupation, under Soviet, British, American and French control.
- Finally, the USSR offered to enter the war against Japan within 3 months of the end of the war in Europe.

■ *TIP* This was a key conference of the Allied powers. Suspicions over Poland and Soviet intentions in eastern Europe began to create conditions for future *Cold War*.

Yeltsin, Boris: statesman, politician and President of the Russian Federation (1991–99).

- He rose to national prominence as communist Mayor of Moscow in 1985, under *Gorbachev*, but was dismissed in 1987 because of pressure from the conservative opposition.
- He was elected President of the Russian Soviet Republic in 1990. His principal achievement was the defeat of a conservative coup against Gorbachev in 1991.
- He replaced Gorbachev following the collapse of the *USSR* at the end of 1991. A controversial President of the Russian Federation, he introduced free-market reforms, but was known for drunkenness and poor health. He handed over the presidency to Vladimir Putin in 1999.

■ *TIP* His involvement in the collapse of the USSR and creation of the Russian Federation made him an important historical figure.

Yom Kippur War, 1973: an Arab–Israeli conflict started by Syria and Egypt, which lasted just 2 months.

- It was organised by the Egyptian premier, Anwar *Sadat*, and its aim was to recapture territory lost to Israel in the *Six Day War* (1967).

- Initial successes of the Egyptian and Syrian forces were soon reversed, mainly through massive American military aid to the Israelis.
- A cease-fire was called after the Israeli Army had crossed the Suez Canal, en route for Cairo, the Egyptian capital.
- The war led to an oil crisis, in which the Arab-dominated cartel OPEC (Organisation of Oil Exporting Countries) quadrupled the price of oil. This caused an economic crisis across the Western world.
- President *Nixon* also threatened the *USSR* with nuclear war if the Soviet Union intervened on the side of the Arabs.
- The territorial situation was restored to what it had been on the eve of war.
- **TIP** The war severely strained the policy of *détente* between the USA and USSR.

Young Italy: a liberal, nationalist organisation created by Giuseppe *Mazzini* in 1832.

- Its aim was to achieve an independent and united Italy, free from foreign domination.
- Mazzini's writings were aimed mainly at Austria, which directly controlled Lombardy and Venetia and had dynastic links with Parma, Modena and Tuscany. In addition, Austria had a military alliance with Naples and Sicily.
- Mazzini's main chance came in 1849, when he helped found the Roman Republic during the 1848–49 Revolutions. The Republic was short-lived and was overthrown by armed forces from France and Spain, which restored the Pope.
- **TIP** Although it failed in its immediate aim, Young Italy inspired a generation of liberals, who helped to unite Italy in 1860.

Young Plan, 1929: a scheme to reduce and reschedule German *reparations* payments.

- It was agreed that Germany should pay 34,500 million gold marks to the Allies in instalments, running up to 1988.
- It stimulated right-wing opposition in Germany, because the government's acceptance of the plan was an acknowledgement of Germany's duty to pay. The leader of the German National People's Party, Alfred Hugenburg, organised a campaign to hold a referendum on the Young Plan.
- **TIP** Participation in the referendum gave a boost to Nazi popularity, following their poor showing in the 1928 *Reichstag* election, where they received 2.8% of the vote and only 12 seats.

Young Turk Revolution, 1908: a liberal reform movement among junior officers in the Ottoman (Turkish) Army.

- Led by Enver Pasha, Ahmed Djemel and Mehmed Talaat, the reformers forced Sultan Abdul Hamid II to introduce parliamentary government open to participation by Christians as well as Muslims.
- A call to defend all Ottoman territory led Austria-Hungary to annex Bosnia-Herzegovina, which it had occupied since 1878. The Austro-Hungarian action started the *Bosnian Crisis* (1908–09).

y

■ *TIP* This movement for reform came too late to save the *Ottoman empire* from collapse following the First World War.

Ypres, Battles of, 1914, 1915, 1917: a series of major clashes in the British sector of the Western Front during the First World War.

● All the battles involved mass infantry attacks, which made little difference to the front line but cost dear in casualties.

● The third battle (also known as Passchendaele) was a British and Canadian attempt to break the German front line in order to capture U-boat bases at Ostend and Zeebrugge. It was fought in the mud of autumn and the British forces lost 200,000 men, killed or wounded.

■ *TIP* These battles were typical of the military stalemate on the Western Front.

zemstvo: a Russian local government body created in 1864 by Tsar *Alexander II*.

- Elected on a property-owning franchise (franchise = right to vote), members of a *zemstvo* had responsibility for road building, education and local health matters.
- They mostly came to be dominated by local landowners from 1881 onwards.
- In 1870 locally elected town *dumas* were also created along similar lines.

■ *TIP* This was the only form of elected government in Russia before creation of the national parliament (State Duma) in 1906. Note that the plural of *zemstvo* is usually written as *zemstva*.

Zhukov, Georgi: a leading Soviet military commander in the Second World War, who captured Berlin in May 1945.

- He rose to prominence during the defence of Moscow (1941).
- He planned the encirclement of the German VIth Army in the Battle of *Stalingrad* (1942) and also took part in the Battle of *Kursk* (1943).
- Demoted by *Stalin* after the war, he again rose to prominence in 1956–57 as a supporter of *Khrushchev*, who made him Minister for Defence, only to dismiss him again in October 1957.

■ *TIP* He was the most successful Soviet military commander in what the Russians remember as the Great Patriotic War.

Zimmermann Telegram, 1917: a secret message passed between the German ambassador in Mexico, Alfred Zimmermann, and Germany, intercepted by British intelligence, which caused the USA to enter the First World War.

- The telegram suggested that, if Mexico entered the war on Germany's side, it would receive Arizona, New Mexico and parts of Texas in return.

■ *TIP* The message understandably caused great resentment in the USA. Along with *unrestricted U-boat warfare*, it helped to push the USA towards war, which was declared against Germany 3 months later.

Zinoviev, Grigori: Russian communist leader, who opposed the *Bolshevik* seizure of power in October 1917 but joined the Council of People's Commissars as head of the Communist International (*Comintern*).

- In 1924 he joined *Kamenev* and *Stalin* to prevent *Trotsky* from succeeding *Lenin*. He was outmanoeuvred by Stalin in 1926, dismissed from the *Politburo* and expelled from the Communist Party in 1927.

- In the Great *Purge*, he was put on trial with Kamenev in secret (1935) and sentenced to 10 years' imprisonment. A year later he faced a Show Trial, which sentenced him to death for attempting to overthrow the *USSR*.
- *TIP* A leading communist from the early days, Zinoviev, like many other Old Bolsheviks, was executed by Stalin in the Great Purge of 1934–39.

Zollparlament, 1867: an attempt by *Bismarck* to form closer economic links with the south German states of Baden, Bavaria, Württemberg and Hesse Darmstadt, following the Prussian victory over Austria in the *Seven Weeks' War* (1866).

- A Customs Parliament was created in the Prussian capital, Berlin, and elected by universal manhood suffrage (one man, one vote).
- It contained representatives from the new *North German Confederation* and the south German states, though the representatives from Bavaria and Württemberg were initially hostile to Prussia.
- Along with a military alliance (1866), the parliament brought the southern states closer to Prussia.
- *TIP* Its formation was a key step towards the unification of Germany.

Zollverein: the German Customs Union, begun in 1818 when Prussia removed all internal trade barriers.

- By 1834 nearly all the *German Confederation* (except Austria) had joined.
- Its domination by Prussia increased with the industrialisation of Germany from the 1850s onwards and greatly assisted the union of German states under Prussian leadership.
- Economic integration was followed in the 1860s by political integration, as a result of the Prussian victory over Austria in the *Seven Weeks' War*.
- *TIP* The *Zollverein* and the industrialisation of Germany were important economic reasons for its eventual unification.

Zürich, Treaty of, 1860: an agreement which brought the Franco–Austrian War of 1859 to an end, following a cease-fire at Villafranca.

- It planned to set up a European congress to discuss the future political structure of Italy.
- The French Emperor, *Napoleon III*, hoped to see Italy divided into four states: Piedmont-Sardinia, the Central Duchies, the Papal States, and Naples and Sicily.
- Napoleon III hoped that France would replace Austria as the dominant *Great Power*.
- The treaty was not implemented, because of a pro-Piedmontese revolution in the Central Duchies and *Cavour*'s invasion of the Papal States.
- *TIP* This was a failed attempt by Napoleon III to limit the unification of Italy.

Appendix
Modules/Units covered in this
Essential Word Dictionary
Advanced Subsidiary (AS)

AQA

Module 1
Revolution and conservatism in France and Europe, 1789–1825
Germany and Russia before the First World War, 1870–1914
Tsarist and revolutionary Russia, 1855–1917
Imperial and Weimar Germany, 1866–1925
Emergence of the superpowers and the New World Order, 1945–62
Origins and consolidation of totalitarian states, 1918–39

Module 3
Europe, 1825–50
The Balkans, 1870–1914
Revolutionary Russia, 1917–29
Germany, *c.*1925–38
Effects of the First World War, 1915–24
Interwar America, 1919–41

Edexcel

Unit 1
Russia in revolution, 1905–17
Seeds of evil: the rise of National Socialism in Germany to 1933
Boom and bust: economy and society in the USA, 1917–33

Unit 2
France in revolution, 1766–94
Road to unification: Italy, *c.*1848–70
Triumph of Bolshevism? Russia, 1918–29
Italy: the rise of fascism, 1918–25
Weimar Germany, 1918–29
Pursuing life and liberty: civil rights in the USA, 1945–68

Unit 3

War and the revolutionary state, 1792–1815
Bismarck and the unification of Germany c.1848–71
Life in Hitler's Germany, 1933–39
Life in the Soviet Union, c.1928–41
Promise and performance: FDR and the New Deal in the USA, 1933–45

OCR

Unit 1

Italian unification, 1848–71
Nazi Germany, 1933–39

Unit 3

Europe, 1789–1849

i)   The French Revolution, 1789–95
ii) Napoleon and Europe, 1799–1815
iii) France, 1814–48
iv) Revolution and repression in Europe, 1848–49

Europe, 1825–90

i)   Italy, 1830–70
ii) Germany, 1862–90
iii) France, 1848–75
iv) Russia, 1825–81

Europe, 1890–1945

i)   Russia, 1890–1945
ii) Causes and impact of the First World War, c.1890–1920
iii) Italy, 1919–45
iv) Germany, 1919–45

Europe and the world, 1919–89

i)   International relations, 1919–39
ii) USSR, 1924–53
iii) Cold War in Europe, 1945–89
iv) Cold War in Asia and the Americas, 1949–75

Advanced (A2)

AQA

Module 4

Nationalism and the state: Europe, 1814–1914

Germany, Russia and the Soviet Union in the nineteenth and twentieth centuries

Russia and the USSR, 1881–1985

Germany, c.1880–1980

Aspects of European and world history, 1900 to the present

Totalitarian ideologies, economic, social and foreign policies, 1848–1956

Economic and social history, 1870–1979

Aspects of domestic issues in the USA, 1877–1989

Module 6

The crowd in the French Revolution, 1789–94

Hitler and the origins of the Second World War, 1933–41

The end of the Soviet Union, c.1968–90

The reunification of Germany, c.1969–90

The United Nations, 1945–89

The Holocaust, 1938–45

The world economy: free trade, protection and European cooperation, 1870–1970

The USA and Vietnam, 1963–73

Edexcel

Unit 4

Bourbons restored: France, 1814–30

Securing the state: Bismarck and Germany, 1871–90

Quest for greatness: fascist Italy, 1924–39

Expansion and aggression: German foreign policy, 1933–39

Europe at war, 1939–45

Stalin and destalinisation, 1945–64

Containing communism? The USA in Asia, 1950–73

Unit 6

Hitler and the Nazi state: power and control, 1933–39

Soviet Union after Lenin, 1924–41

Cold War and *détente*, 1945–90

OCR

Unit 4

Napoleon I

Bismarck and the unification of Germany, 1858–71

America: boom and bust, 1920–41

Lenin and the consolidation of Bolshevik power, 1917–29

Britain and Germany, 1933–39

Causes of the Cold War, 1944–49

Unit 5

Changing nature of warfare, 1792–1918

Challenge of German nationalism, 1815–1919

Russian dictatorship, 1855–1956